# The New America:

# The America

# of the

# Moo-Shoo Burrito

# The New America:

# The America

# of the

# Moo-Shoo Burrito

# Stan Perea

with Cheryl A. Smith

HIS Ministries Publications

Denver, Colorado

For information or permissions, address:
HIS Ministries Publications
6820 Osage
Denver, CO 80221

*The New America: The America of the Moo-Shoo Burrito*
may be purchased in bulk for education, business, or sales
promotional use at discounted rates. For information
please write HIS Ministries Publications, 6820 Osage,
Denver, CO 80221, hisministries@earthlink.net, or visit
the website at www.HISMinistries.com.

First Edition

ISBN 0-9760274-0-2

*Interior design by Graphiti Girls*

# Dedication

To my Father, who taught me how to live,

To my Mother, who taught me how to love,

And especially to my wife, Glenda, who has shown me true love and who has allowed me to love her for the best thirty-seven years of my life.

# Table of Contents

# Preface

It is time we had an honest discussion about immigration and cultural differences in America without resorting to name-calling or hate talk. God has determined that this is where we shall live, and we must learn to live together with the ability to debate and resolve issues that are critical to the future of the country we all love.

We must set policy in this country for the long term and not merely based on the votes we will receive in the next election. We owe it to our children and grandchildren to help them translate culture and to model for them an inclusive America "indivisible, with liberty and justice for all."

I have attempted to describe an America that while unrecognizable to many, and consequently frightening to them, is an America that is ever-improving and changing for the better; an America that is being given new life by the immigrants who are coming here with hopes and dreams for their families, just as the immigrants before them have done; an America that is becoming more Hispanic and more Asian every day!

I want to thank my wife, Glenda, for putting up with my collection of materials and my talk about this book for the past fifteen years. I thank my daughter, Amy, for proofreading draft after draft, my friend Becky for doing a final proofreading, and my friend Patricia for encouraging me and assuring me that I have something to say. I thank Dr. Brent Cruz, Dr. Pete Menconi, and my good friend of many years Dr. Gordon England for their counsel, criticism, and help. I thank my daughter-in-law Angela for her help with the cover design. A special thank you to Cheryl Smith; without her organization and prodding, this book would still be rattling around in my mind and heart.

I hope you will find in these pages some handles for the changes that you have been seeing taking place all around you.

Stan Perea
August, 2004

# Introduction:

## The Moo-Shoo Burrito Culture

N othing endures but change." So said Heraclitus, the philosopher who posited that you cannot step into the same river twice. We see change all around us in our cities and suburbs. The old-fashioned mom-and-pop store on the corner is torn down to make room for a "strip mall," which is later demolished to make a parking lot for the shopping mall, which is later turned back into an outdoor mall with picturesque little mom-and-pop shops (which, by the way, are franchised all over the country in case you want one).

Even more striking than these physical changes, though, is the change in our culture. The 2000 Census revealed a growing number of non-white groups, particularly Hispanics, in America. An *Economist* article states, "Somewhere in the past ten years, the number of Californians who describe themselves as white fell behind the number who describe themselves as something else. To put it in shorthand, 'whites are no longer a majority.'"[1]

We could, of course, just ascribe this phenomenon to California as we have with New Age spirituality, homosexuality, and miniskirts. After all, what "they" do out there has nothing to do with the rest of the country.

However, as Victor Davis Hanson notes in *Mexifornia*, California is "traditionally the early warning sign to the rest of the country."[2] As California goes, so goes the nation.

Two events were signposts to me of the changing culture. The first was a wedding I performed several years ago. The groom was a Catholic Asian who had been raised in Australia. The bride's family was Jewish. Her brother had married an Indian woman. The photograph of the wedding party shows a mix of colors and cultures. If we could listen, we would hear a mix of accents. No longer can we assume that a white boy will marry a white girl.

The other signpost occurred in the late 1980s. I had just started seminary, and my personal life was already in the midst of change. One day I went to lunch with a client in the newly burgeoning suburb of Highlands Ranch, Colorado. I had moo-shoo pork, which was pretty spicy and was served with what I later learned were called pancakes, although they weren't anything like the pancakes my wife makes and serves with syrup. I mentioned to the owner how good the moo-shoo would be as a burrito, with tortillas instead of the pancakes. About a year later, the Moo-Shoo Burrito was on the menu. The combination of these two flavors represents the two fastest growing populations in America, the Hispanic and the Asian.

Church of the Rockies in Denver, Colorado, the Reformed Church in America church I pastored until January 2004, reflected these populations as well. A Korean church held services in our building on Saturdays, and in 2003 we started a Spanish-language congregation on Sunday afternoons in addition to our regular services on Sunday morning. One Saturday evening, the three congregations came together at the church for a concert and potluck dinner. We had hamburgers and hotdogs, the Koreans brought eggrolls, and the Latinos brought Mexican food. One man smothered his eggrolls with salsa and said,

# Introduction

"Pastor, these are great Korean taquitos."

Americans had heard quite a bit about salsa replacing ketchup as America's favorite condiment. Lately, ketchup, which never needed much advertising to be a condiment bestseller, has become #1 again due to strong advertising campaigns and some innovative changes, including *green* ketchup for kids. Now, tortillas are starting to replace white bread. "According to market research company IRI, supermarket sales of white bread dropped 0.6 percent in 2002 from the year before, while tortilla sales grew 11 percent. Private-label tortilla sales jumped a whopping 26 percent. Retail and food-service sales of tortillas have nearly doubled in a six-year period to $5.2 billion in 2002, up from $2.8 billion in 1996."[3]

That's the New America – the America of the Korean taquito and the moo-shoo burrito, salsa vs. ketchup, and tortillas vs. bread. And this is just the surface of the changes that are occurring!

Some are fearful of the changes and have suggested that America adopt more stringent immigration laws and a stricter border policy, in effect pulling the welcome mat back inside. When our Lady Liberty said, "Give me your poor, your tired, your huddled masses yearning to breathe free," she didn't actually mean *all* of them.

Others are suggesting that if we continue to let people in, they must assimilate to "our" way of life and "our" values. We should stop putting up signs in English and Spanish. Pass English-only laws. Let them, or make them, learn English. After all, it's our country. We're the melting pot, so melt!

The problem, of course, is that what worked a century ago no longer works today. Assimilation doesn't work anymore because there is no longer a single cohesive America to assimilate into. At one time, we – and the rest of the world – were secluded. When people came to America, they broke ties with their homeland and said good-bye to family and close friends, in many cases for the rest of their lives. With today's global village, that's no longer the case. Technology has made the world smaller, less segregated. Immigrants can turn on the television and see news from around the world. They can e-mail the family and friends they left back in the homeland, keeping them a part of the family, of that particular community. With low airfares, they can travel home – something that our immigrant ancestors could not have dreamed of. They can now live in this country and never have to learn English in order to get by, again something that was unheard of in the past.

America is changing, and there is simply no way to return to what America was before. This doesn't mean, however, that we are headed down the tubes, or that the changes are necessarily for the worse.

How many times did we as children listen to our elders say, "When I was your age," only to in turn repeat that same phrase to our children or grandchildren? Inherent in the tired idiom is the belief that the older way is better, that change is always for the worse. In 1829, Martin Van Buren, then governor of New York, wrote the following letter to President Andrew Jackson, predicting the physical and economic doom that certain changes would have upon American society:

> The canal system of this country is being threatened by the spread of a new form of transportation known as "railroads." The federal government must preserve the canals for the following reasons:

> One. If canal boats are supplanted by "railroads," serious unemployment will result. Captains, cooks, drivers, hostlers,

repairmen, lock tenders will be left without means of livelihood, not to mention the numerous farmers now employed in growing hay for horses.

Two. Boat builders would suffer and towline, whip and harness makers would be left destitute.

Three. Canal boats are absolutely essential to the defense of the United States. In the event of the expected trouble with England, the Erie Canal would be the only means by which we would ever move the supplies so vital to waging modern war.

As you may well know, Mr. President, "railroad" carriages are pulled at the enormous speed of fifteen miles per hour by "engines" which, in addition to endangering life and limb of passengers, roar and snort their way through the countryside, setting fire to crops, scaring the livestock and frightening our women and children. The Almighty certainly never intended that people should travel at such breakneck speed.

Today, the letter seems quaint, and we smile at its naiveté. The attitude toward change, however, hasn't – well – changed. The doomsayers are still out in force, clanging their bells to warn the people. Change, however, is neutral. What isn't neutral is our management of change. How do we handle the changes that are occurring? King Whitney, Jr., president of Personnel Laboratory, Inc., understood the dynamics of change. To his staff, he said, "Change has considerable psychological impact on the human mind. To the fearful it is threatening because it means that things may get worse. To the hopeful it is encouraging because things may get better. To the confident it is inspiring because *the challenge exists to make things better*."[4]

The book you are reading answers that challenge to help make things better. Hispanics have a saying: "Cuando se revuelve la agua, qual quier bagre aparece como pescado." "When the water gets muddy, any old catfish looks like a trout." We are indeed living in times of muddy waters. As Bob Dylan once sang, "The times they are a-changin'." I am confident that the changes, already and still occurring, can make society better, if we work to make things better. Change can mean great opportunity, if we view it that way. This book was written as a way to not only examine the changes, but also to move toward better management of the changes, toward seizing the opportunities presented.

As mentioned above, when change comes, it is natural to fight for the status quo. It is natural for people in power to fight to remain in power. Chapter one will discuss the Individualistic/Enmeshed model I use to demonstrate the attitudes prevalent in all aspects of our society, including the fight for power by both the powerful and the powerless.

With the rise in minority populations, America is fast becoming a land where no people-group will enjoy majority status. This indeed is the New America. What these multicultural changes are and how they are coming about will be the subject of chapter two.

Chapters three through nine will look at a variety of issues in the New America, beginning with the family. The model will be discussed in relation to each issue. Each of these chapters offers questions at the end to encourage discussion and further study. The final chapter will suggest ways to deal with the two extremes and how to move to the middle where America can best serve all interests.

One note on terminology. A great deal of discussion is currently going on about what term should describe this brown population. Latino and Hispanic are not interchangeable. Latinos are those Spanish-speaking people from the Americas south of the United States and would include Mexicans and Puerto Ricans. Hispanics are those of Spanish descent, the peoples of the Iberian Peninsula. When I am referring specifically to United States Census figures, I will use the term "Hispanic," because that is what is designated on the census form. If I am referring specifically to one ethnic group, I will use the appropriate designation of Mexican, Spanish, Cuban, South American, Central American, or Puerto Rican. For all other usages, I will use Latino(a), a term which is rising in popularity and seems to be the future term for this large population. No offense is meant by the use of any of these terms.

Every time I have shared with others the changes in America and how these changes impact us, as well as the Individualistic/Enmeshed model, I have received surprised looks, enthusiastic comments, and a flood of further information. Everyone recognizes themselves in the model as well as their communities and the society at large. It is my hope that you will encounter yourself in these pages, and will be, in the words of King Whitney Jr., inspired and challenged to make an impact for a better world.

## Notes

[1] "The Golden State Turns Brown," *The Economist*, April 7, 2001.

[2] Victor Davis Hanson, *Mexifornia: A State of Becoming* (San Francisco: Encounter Books, 2003).

[3] Barry Shlachter, "Tortillas Wrap Up a Growing Share of Bread Market," *The Denver Post*, Nov. 16, 2003, 10K.

[4] Quoted in *Wall Street Journal*, June 7, 1967. Emphasis mine.

# Chapter 1

## The Individualistic/Enmeshed Model:
## Finding the Balance

Ask one hundred people what the good life is and you will no doubt get one hundred different answers. Many books have been written on the subject, and it promises to be a question that will be debated well into the future.

When Aristotle sought to define a good life, he began with his theory of virtue and stated that in order to live a good life, a man or woman must be a person of virtue. To put his theory in the simplest terms, what is needed for virtue is balance. Each virtue, he said, has two extremes at opposite ends of a spectrum, and virtue is found in the middle of those extremes. To give the most common example, consider the virtue of courage. At one extreme is cowardice; at the other extreme is rashness or foolhardiness. Courage is acting in a manner that is toward the center, neither too rash nor too cowardly. Wisdom, the supreme virtue, is knowing where that middle ground is. As Euripides said, "The best and safest thing is to keep a balance in your life, … If you can do that, and live that way, you are really a wise man."

In a similar vein, psychoanalyst Erik Erikson, who in the 1950s was working on a theory of identity crisis, developed his eight stages of psychosocial development. His belief was that each stage in life is characterized by a conflict between harmonious and disharmonius elements that must be resolved by the individual in order to grow and achieve a sense of identity. This identity crisis is inevitable; when the environment in which people live changes or makes new demands on them, conflicts come up, forcing crisis resolution, and, if resolved correctly, forging identity.

## The Model

I believe that we can apply these two theories to social systems as well. In the Individualistic/Enmeshed model, shown on the opposite page, the conflict is between the individual at one extreme and the community at the other. There is nothing wrong *per se* with either of these concepts. Each person needs to be an individual and each individual needs community. Taken to the extreme, though, individuals, and societies, may become Individualistic, while communities may become Enmeshed. At the extremes, then, each position is untenable at best and destructive at worst. Both the Individualistic and Enmeshed extremes are dysfunctional and pathological; wisdom, as Aristotle taught, is needed to find the mid-point between the extremes.

Now, I know that there are people reading this who are at the Individualistic extreme and are thinking right now, "But not me. I have community. I play golf with my friends, and we're a community." And there are others at the Enmeshed extreme who are saying, "But not us. We allow people to be individual." And both are true, but only to a limited extent. The question is, do you regularly interact

# THE INDIVIDUALISTIC / ENMESHED MODEL

Individualistic        Wholeness        Enmeshed

(Individual)        (Community)

Individual more important than the
   community
Success measured by:
   Power
   Wealth
Rewards competition
Politically conservative
Education: importance of the degree
Capitalism: Bootstrap Theory
The Corona Loner/Marlboro Man

Wholeness is where
each extreme finds
community with the
other. Wholeness is
being at home and
comfortable with
both sides.

Community more important than
   the individual
Success measured by:
   Relationships
   Connectedness
Punish competition
Politically liberal
Education: importance of learning
Socialism
The Coors Fiesta

Each extreme is pathological.
Wholeness if found at the center.

with people who aren't like you? Let me come back to this question after we've looked at the extremes.

## Individualistic

Look at the model on the preceding page, which will be used in the succeeding chapters. On the Individualistic side is the America that we're familiar with, even if we don't personally live it. It's John Wayne's America – "rugged individualism," never needing or asking for help, riding off into the sunset rather than staying and becoming part of the community he's just rescued. The motto for this America is "pull yourself up by your own bootstraps."

The Individualistic side is characterized by competition and a drive to succeed. Success is measured by power and money. Education is important for the degree that entitles one to power and money. Learning doesn't matter as much as having that little piece of paper. Parents are deemed successful if they raise children who fit into this model of success. No longer is someone deemed successful simply by virtue of being a good person or of staying married until death or of fulfilling the obligations of a job for which one is ill-suited. George Bailey of the film *It's a Wonderful Life* may be the "richest man in town" because of his friendships, but no one seriously thinks of George as successful or uses him as a career role model.

Gary Wederspahn, a speaker who has conducted cross-cultural training programs for hundreds of global executives and such diverse corporations as General Motors, Coca Cola, and Merrill Lynch, notes, "Proverbs and popular sayings are capsules that contain highly condensed bits of a culture's values and beliefs." He believes that those who want a glimpse into the attitudes and values of American culture should examine its popular sayings. About the saying, "pull yourself up by your own bootstraps," he says:

Related to our optimism and belief in self-reliance is our assumption that a person's success or failure is almost entirely due to his or her own efforts and abilities. We tend to reject the idea that fate and external circumstances are forces that determine one's future. This belief in self-determination partially explains why our social welfare programs are relatively limited compared to most other industrialized nations.[1]

As Wederspahn states, this assumption is based on a belief in self-reliance, reflected in such proverbs as "stand on your own two feet" and "God helps those who help themselves." Belief in self-reliance came along with the frontier expansion of America. With families starting to become mobile in the expansion westward, people became more isolated. They had to depend on themselves rather than on a community. This self-reliance continued on through the Depression years when lack of money demanded generalization. Specialists in any field weren't affordable, so you learned to fix your own car, build your own fence, and repair your own appliances. While in some ways we have lost respect for the actual skills these activities demand, we still value highly the attitude of "I can do it myself." Wederspahn notes, "We had to rely on ourselves and gradually turned this necessity into a virtue."

Most parents still raise their children to be self-reliant and not depend on others. We have been taught to consider it a weakness when older people can no longer care for themselves or live alone.

This self-reliance epitomizes the Individualistic extreme of the model. Now let's look at the Enmeshed extreme.

## Enmeshed

If a John Wayne western typifies the Individualistic extreme, Nia Vardalos' 2002 hit film *My Big Fat Greek Wedding* epitomizes the Enmeshed extreme. The important concept in Enmeshed is family. There is a very definite division between insiders and outsiders, and if you're not an insider, you might not ever become one. On the extreme side, it is difficult to leave the family, and you're almost considered a traitor if you do. As Michael Corleone says to his brother in the film *The Godfather*, "Fredo, you're my older brother and I love you, but don't ever take sides with anyone against the family again. Ever." We probably all felt that way to some extent when we were growing up. I could insult my younger brother and push him around, but don't let anyone else try to get away with that!

Rick Manzanares of the Colorado Historical Society museum at Fort Garland wrote about the community aspect of the settlers of the San Luis Valley in Colorado. "You had the village system that was very family and communal oriented. The plaza was built for a reason, to keep the Indians from coming in and attacking. The farm system and the *acequia* system all depended very much on everybody cooperating, because there wasn't a lot of government. You had to have this communal system for existence."[2]

Many people, particularly those who have grown up under the Individualistic extreme, believe that the Enmeshed extreme doesn't value success. This reflects a misreading of the culture. Success is simply defined in different ways. Let me give you an example.

Several years ago, while I was working as a consultant on cross-cultural issues, a large corporation in Alamosa, Colorado, hired me to determine where it was going wrong. It was offering good wages and many overtime opportunities to anyone who wanted it in order to get the company's production up. The problem, as I explained to the managers, is that the population of Alamosa is largely Latino, and while Latinos value money, they value time more. I suggested that the company hire more people at reduced hours so that people could spend more time with their families preparing for winter (cutting wood, working their small farms). The company followed my recommendation and was able to get production up – something it valued – and the workers got more time off – something they valued.

A pair of beer commercials will highlight the differences in the Individualistic/Enmeshed model. The commercial for Corona beer portrays the Individualistic extreme. A white, thirty-something man, obviously successful because of the cell phone and other business accoutrements, relaxes alone on a beach. Gulls swoop overhead, the water is bright blue, the solitude is peaceful, enticing. (For the previous generation, the exemplar was the Marlboro Man. He was an unemotional loner; nothing could tie him down; he needed no one or nothing as long as he had his smoke.) More than simply an individual, the Corona man, like the Marlboro Man before him, is Individualistic.

The commercials for Coors beer, on the other hand, depict the Enmeshed extreme. Break out a bottle of Coors and let the fiesta begin! There's people and music and dancing – you're never alone if you have a Coors in your hand. More than simply a community, the party is Enmeshed. Corona Beer is trying to sell to the "white American" population while Coors is trying to gain a larger share of the Latino market. The marketing people know their audiences, and they know what appeals to both extremes.

# A Personal Dysfunction and Discovery

As stated earlier, each end of the model is dysfunctional. Each end needs to move toward the center in order to find wholeness. The pragmatist philosopher William James put it this way, "The community stagnates without the impulse of the individual. The impulse dies away without the sympathy of the community." Both are necessary components of our society. I have found this to be the case in my own life and in my own movement between Individualistic and Enmeshed.

I was born and raised in Antonito, a small town in Southern Colorado, the middle child of six boys and four girls. We were a poor family in one of the poorest counties in the country. My job every night was to cut out cardboard for our shoes, because our shoes had holes in them and cardboard lasted only a day. Although we were poor, we were happy, and we were never on welfare. Dad worked county road maintenance, worked as a bartender evenings and weekends, and farmed sixty acres. We grew grain and raised hogs, bartering for chili and potatoes.

Growing up, I learned from our society that to be a Mexican was to be a "lazy Mexican" or a "dirty Mexican," as though the noun always demanded a pejorative adjective. Being Mexican was a cause of shame, of dishonor. When I was young, we hid our food, because we were ashamed of eating Mexican dishes. A meter reader used to come from the Public Service Company every month, and he always came at dinnertime. I remember my brothers and sisters saying, "Mr. Winkle is coming! Hide the tortillas!" It's ironic that now we stand in line at Taco Bell to eat tortillas that aren't nearly as tasty as the ones in my memory!

I attended school in Antonito, Colorado, where we were punished for speaking Spanish, even though we didn't know English. Because the county had gone broke at one time and the schools were going to shut down, the Catholic Church brought in nuns to teach in order to keep the school open. When the county got back on its feet, they realized what good teachers the nuns were, so they hired them, and they lived in a house built on school property. The nuns would hit us across the fingers with a ruler if we were caught speaking Spanish. The thinking back then – which isn't much different from today, in some respects – was, "you need to learn English, because this is America." So we became fluently bilingual, *fast*, but we never gave up Spanish and still spoke it at home. My parents were ashamed to speak English because they had trouble pronouncing the words. They didn't need to worry; the nuns couldn't speak any Spanish, and they butchered our names. I grew up in Conejos (coe-*nay*-hoes) County, but the nuns pronounced it "Connie Joes."

There were only two or three whites in the entire high school, and we considered them as "one of us." I had classes with them and played football with them. It was one of the first places, though, that I started encountering cultural differences, and began noticing the dissimilarities between us. I'd go spend the night at the resort-ranch of one of the kids, and it was a different lifestyle. What he called "freedom," I called disconnectedness in his family. His family tended to communicate through notes. "I'm going to the party," his note to them would read. Or they'd leave him a note, "We're out to dinner. We'll be back later." In his family, everyone had their own path, their own thing to do.

I graduated in 1966, came to Denver, and got a job at the post office. I drove back to Antonito every weekend and would go to the college to look for girls. On one of those trips, I met my future wife, Glenda. I was 17, and she was 18. Although I had started noticing cultural differences when I was in high school, dating Glenda was when culture shock really set in. Glenda's background is German, and she's blonde and blue-eyed. Her parents treated me very well. They ran a restaurant in Lyons. They were nice people, and when I'd go up there, I would have steaks with them after they had closed for the night. Then I asked them if I could marry their daughter. Her father said no. In the first place, he said, you're Catholic, and in the second place, you're Mexican. That was the first time I learned that it's worse to be Catholic than Mexican! (Back then, the divide was pretty severe between Catholic and Protestant. If you were a Catholic and went into a Protestant church, it meant you were going to hell. Bill, my best friend in Antonito, was a Presbyterian, and he wasn't allowed to go to the Catholic Church with me. Whenever we spent the night together, though, he went to my church and I went to his, so even then the two of us were pushing the envelope.)

Through many talks, Glenda's parents accepted me and my ideas. (In fact, they and the rest of Glenda's family became staunch supporters of my ministry.) Glenda and I met in January and were married in April. A year or so later, I attended the University of Colorado through a Latino scholarship called the Migrant Action program. I quit the post office, which made my family angry, because I was quitting a government job with a retirement program; Latinos just didn't get those kinds of jobs, and yet I quit to go to the university.

The American Dream was calling me, and I pushed toward Individualistic success with everything I had. I became the director of the Migrant Action program and spent four years at CU Boulder participating in anti-war demonstrations and Chicano movement demonstrations. I graduated in 1973 with a degree in accounting, which was unheard of at the time. I took a position with Peat Marwick Mitchell and Company, which was then the largest CPA firm in the world. They offered me a position in any office

I wanted, so I took Tucson because I had family there. There was a Latino-owned bank there, one of the first in the country, and that became a client of mine. A year later, I set up my own firm and became the controller of the bank.

In 1979, I sold the firm and moved back to Denver. I was recruited by Denver Community Development Corporation to be Director of Business Development, where I brought in millions of dollars worth of federal funds to do community development. We built shopping centers and warehouses, set up job training programs, and provided jobs for Latinos in the inner city. I was there three years and set up my own CPA firm. I had offices in Washington DC, Tucson, and Alamosa. I was living at the Individualistic extreme, and I was having a blast.

In 1985, though, my world started to crash. The associates in the firm were suing each other and suing me, buying each other's stock; everyone wanted a bigger portion of the pie. At the time, Glenda and I were living in Alamosa on a sixteen-acre ranch with quarter horses for our three kids, the kids I never saw. I was traveling to Denver so much that I had a town home in a west Denver suburb for when I couldn't make it back home. I rarely saw my family. I thought I was providing for them by just giving them money. The problem was that I never gave them my time. Glenda asked me to move out, so I planned to move permanently into the townhome and hire someone to do my cleaning and laundry.

Although I didn't know it at the time, God was preparing a path for me. Larry Jaramillo, a friend and co-worker, was a Christian, and he used to travel with me once a week. I would come home late at night from partying, and he would be reading his Bible. I can remember many nights when we'd go into our separate bedrooms, I'd look over and he'd be on his knees praying. No matter what came at him, he always seemed calm; he had a certain peace in his life

27

that I knew was missing from mine. He'd go into his room with the Bible, and I'd go into mine with the *Wall Street Journal, The Economist*, and all of my business books. He used to say to me while holding up a Bible, "Perea, if you ever gave up all of those books for *this* Book, you could be dangerous." He was always praying for me, and I desperately needed those prayers.

On a Saturday morning in 1986, I knew it was over. Glenda and I were getting divorced. I took off on US-285 from Denver heading for Alamosa to pick up my things. I was tired of the burden I was carrying, weary of being the first Latino to do this or the top Latino to do that. In 1984, I had gotten an award for Businessman of the Year from the Small Business Administration. Here it was two years later; my marriage was over, my business was bankrupt. My life was falling apart.

That Saturday morning, near Bailey, Colorado, on a two-lane stretch of highway, an 18-wheel semi-tractor trailer was coming at me, and I turned the steering wheel in front of it.

Until the day I die, I will remember that the wheel turned in my hands, but the car kept going straight. I pulled off the side of the road and spent two and a half hours just sobbing. I said to the Lord, "I don't know what you have for me, but my life is rotten. I will work for you the rest of my life as hard as I worked for me the first 37 years of my life."

I had looked at my life and thought the answer was going to be education, so I got a degree. I thought it was going to be money, so I made more than I knew what to do with. I thought it was going to be in politics, so I raised money for Henry Cisneros, the mayor of San Antonio, for Tony Anaya, the governor of New Mexico, for Bruce Babbitt to become governor of Arizona, and for Frederico Peña to become mayor of Denver. I was co-treasurer for the San Luis Valley in Colorado on the campaign for Roy

Romer's first race for governor. In other words, I was living the Individualistic dream, but it was killing me.

That day on my way to Alamosa, trying to end my life in front of a semi, I came face to face with Jesus Christ. He was the answer. For me, it didn't matter what came at me for the rest of my life; my life would be centered on Jesus Christ. It was a very powerful experience for me and changed everything.

For the first time in my life, I felt that there was no longer a burden that I was carrying. For several years, I hung on the wall in my study my Businessman of the Year award next to my certificate of bankruptcy as a reminder that the Individualistic extreme wasn't the answer. Neither were the expectations and life at the Enmeshed extreme. My answer had come on an almost-deserted stretch of highway.

## The Challenge

I grew up in Antonito on the Enmeshed side of the model. Getting a college degree really moved me away from that. To become a CPA, however, I overcompensated and went completely over to the other side, the Individualistic side. I became "uppity" in my community, a sell-out because I had a degree, possibly a sell-out because I had a white wife (another first in my family, although not the last).

Once during my Individualistic days, I went to a family reunion down in Antonito. People were taking tents; Glenda and the kids went down in a motor home; I flew in from Texas. All of these people were in shorts, tennis shoes, and t-shirts, and all I had with me for the weekend were two 3-piece suits, wing tip shoes, and an extra clean white shirt. I realized then just how far to the Individualistic extreme I had gone. There wasn't a lot of connection in my family for me. They were still connected and were having discussions about people I didn't even remember. But I was as disconnected as anyone on the Individualistic side can be.

I've lived at both extremes of the model. A lot of my thinking, reflected in a large measure in this book, is a reminder to myself of where I've been and how to find wholeness in the middle. I need to be able to connect on both sides. A good friend and co-laborer Gordon England once said about me that I had the ability to walk with kings and peasants, that I was as comfortable with the CEOs in the boardroom as I was with the poor in the inner city. That's because I've been in both places. I can identify with the struggles each side faces and the joys each side brings.

Both places have strengths to recommend them; both sides can learn from the other if they are willing to give up the power struggles. That's the challenge, and it is on that road that wisdom is found.

I asked toward the beginning of this chapter whether you interact with people who aren't like you. Do you? Even the insane find community within the insane asylum. But do you relate to people on the other end of the extreme? Do you, as someone on the Individualistic side, find community with those who don't speak English or with those who live in an economically different neighborhood than you? How often do you, as someone on the Enmeshed side, find community with those who aren't "familia" or with those who hear the beat of a different drummer? Can bridges be built between community and individualism?

The next chapter will examine in depth how the country is shifting between Individualistic and Enmeshed because of changing demographics. It's important to note now, however, what our attitudes are toward this change. Most people think the country is going to hell. Books like Victor Davis Hanson's *Mexifornia* mourn the California that has been lost, a California that will never return because of immigration. The Christian Coalition and other right-leaning groups look nostalgically to the 1950s and make efforts, politically, spiritually, and culturally, to travel back in time. Those on the Individualistic side sense that they are losing power and so fight to maintain the status quo. We may be like Frodo in *The Lord of the Rings* who when trouble befalls him says to Gandalf the wizard, "I wish the ring had never come to me . . . I wish none of this had happened." Gandalf's reply is one that we can all learn from, that speaks to our urge to maintain the status quo. He says, "So do all who live to see such times, but that is not for them to decide. All we have to decide is what to do with the time that is given to us."

Like Frodo, we may be looking at the present shift from Individualistic to Enmeshed as a catastrophe. However, according to Erik Erikson, the crisis that leads to growth isn't a catastrophe but a turning point toward "enhanced potential."

## Notes

[1] Gary M. Wederspahn, "American Sayings: Foreigners' Windows Into US Culture," 5. Wederspahn's articles and book may be found at www.intercultural-help.com.

[2] Dick Foster, "Tradition lives in San Luis Valley," *Rocky Mountain News,* Nov. 16, 1999, 4A.

# Chapter 2

## The Face of the New America

Whether you're describing someone to a friend or giving a police report or simply looking at someone to solidify his or her name in your mind, the person's face is probably the single most important identifying factor. It matters to us what we look like, which is why plastic surgery practices are booming. If America is changing as rapidly and as definitively as I have suggested, what does the New America look like?

According to the Census Bureau, Hispanic and Asian populations are the fastest growing populations in the country. By 2025, Hispanics will comprise 17 percent of the total population; many estimate that number will reach 25 percent by 2050, making Hispanics the largest minority in a country that no longer has a majority. Some states, such as California, already bear this out.

We are, in fact, seeing the greatest surge of immigrant growth since the end of the nineteenth and the beginning of the twentieth centuries, when Irish, Germans, Italians, and other Europeans crowded our harbors. At that time, an English Jew named Israel Zangwill wrote his play, "The Melting Pot," which portrayed an America that welcomed immigrants, promising them freedom, democracy, and perhaps most important, Americanization. Each person had the promise, no matter what heritage, of becoming an American, and therefore having access to the greatest thing of all: the American Dream.

These questions with this second great wave are, Are we still a melting pot? Were we ever? Can the varied people coming to our country now assimilate? Or will our country become ever more splintered? What about the diverse races that are already here? Is there, or should there still be, the ideal of the American Dream?

The questions are complex, and each side offers persuasive arguments for what America is and what it should become. The two most common answers for what America is becoming is that America is a melting pot or that America is a salad bowl. (Of one thing we all can agree: Americans are obsessed with food!)

## Melting Pot?

On one side of the issue, we have people saying that we are becoming more and more blended, that our melting pot has finally and truly melted. This can be borne out by statistics that show that intermarriage is becoming more frequent. The 1990 census showed that over 80 percent of Arab Americans marry non-Arab spouses, implying "diminishing ethnic identification." Consider these statistics from the more current 2000 Census:

> Roughly 30 percent of second-generation Latinos and Asians now wed people from outside their own racial groups. Mixed-race births in California have grown from 40,000 in 1980 to more than 70,000 annually; one out of every seven babies born in the Golden State in 1997 had parents of different races.

> This unprecedented mixing alone guarantees
> the development of an increasingly blended
> culture, not only for Latinos and Asians in
> particular but for young Americans as a
> whole.[1]

The Census Bureau projects that by 2050, the percentage of the population that claims mixed ancestry will rise. "Among Asian Americans, the percentage able to claim some other ancestry in addition to Asian is expected to reach 36%; for Native Americans 89%; for whites 21%; for blacks 14%; and for Hispanics 45%."[2]

The United States Census questionnaire itself is acknowledging that we are a more blended nation. For the first time in census history, respondents to the 2000 Census were allowed to select more than one of six racial designations. Previously, if a child had one white parent and one black parent, what did that child put down as race? Now, that child doesn't have to choose one ancestry over the other, but can select both.

Assimilation has always been a part of American culture. With the rise of the New America, however, what does assimilation mean, and who is assimilating into whom?

> All this mixing suggests that the traditional
> definition of "assimilation into the American
> mainstream" – meaning to lose one's ethnic
> and racial identity in the process of
> becoming more Anglo – may lose its
> meaning. "Assimilation has always been
> more of a confluence of different factors,
> and it's going to be more so in the future,"
> says the Census Bureau's [Jorge] del Pinal.
> "Just look at the influence of Hispanic

immigrants on popular culture now. Nachos have become one of the most popular food snacks. People drink lime with their beer. Salsa is everywhere. The future is going to be a big mixing of cultural influences like that."[3]

Simply put, there is no longer a single American culture to assimilate into.

## Salad Bowl?

Other research seems to bear out that we are not a melting pot and never have been. Rather than a melting pot, we are more like a tossed salad with bits and pieces of carrot, croutons, and cabbage with maybe a tomato thrown in for color. David Brooks writes in *The Atlantic Monthly*, "We don't really care about diversity all that much in America, even though we talk about it a great deal. . . . Instead what I have seen all around the country is people making strenuous efforts to group themselves with people who are basically like themselves."[4]

As Brooks notes, because we are no longer tied to factories or farms, because mobility has enlarged our choices, most people will "search for places to live on the basis of cultural affinity. Once they find a town in which people share their values, they flock there, and reinforce whatever was distinctive about the town in the first place."

Neighborhoods, though, still seem to be segregated, which makes the United States look diverse when looked at as a whole (or as one person put it, from an airplane), but like a tossed salad when looked at in smaller blocks. "According to an analysis of the 2000 census data, the 1990s saw only a slight increase in the racial integration of neighborhoods in the United States. The number of middle-class and upper-middle-class African-American families is rising, but for whatever reasons – racism, psychological comfort – these families tend to congregate in predominantly black neighborhoods."[5]

The trend is similar, although with smaller numbers, for Hispanic growth. While Hispanic immigrants are spreading throughout the nation, "they are living in increasingly segregated neighborhoods in cities where they are the largest minority." In many metro areas, Hispanics are more segregated now than they were in 1990. The census utilizes a "segregation index" to measure the percentage of ethnic people who would have to move in order to be fully integrated with non-Hispanic whites. So, in Dallas, for example, "where Hispanics now make up 23% of the population, the index went from 50.6 to 56.5. That means that 56.5% of Hispanics would have to move to less-Hispanic neighborhoods to be fully integrated with whites." The percentage on average for blacks is 68 percent.[6]

Some of the reason for segregation is an emphasis on multiculturalism. While the goal at one time may have been to foster more diversity by celebrating what is different about each culture, what has happened is that people have tended to congregate with others like themselves. Multiculturalism has emphasized the differences to the point of eliminating similarities. Sharon Noguchi believes this to be a dangerous trend:

> Professor Giles Conwill of Morehouse College said, "A group's decision to separate is simply an affirmation of its own cultural identity." That is true. And that is bad. . . . cultural affirmation also can mean cultural exclusion. . . . Separation is dangerous thinking, not just because of the obvious

appeal to racists. This country of immigrants and old-timers will thrive only with integration. The world is full of places where ethnicities are thrown together and, after affirming their cultural – or religious or ethnic or linguistic – identities for centuries, violently turn upon one another. We do not want to be a Northern Ireland or Bosnia or Rwanda.[7]

So which is it? Are we as a nation like a tossed salad of segregation? Or are we a melting pot, racially becoming so blended that in five years time, none of us will be able to claim "racial purity"? I believe the answer to both of these questions is yes, while at the same time no. Before I explain what I mean by that seeming equivocation, let's look at one more feature of our new face, living out the American Dream.

## The American Dream

Life, liberty, and the pursuit of happiness, right? While the framers of our Constitution may have had such lofty ideals as freedom and democracy in mind while drafting the Constitution, the American Dream came to mean something different as time went on. The American Dream at its most simple and well known is two parents with 2.5 children, a house with a white picket fence surrounding a well-manicured lawn, a dog, and a car. Today, we can modify it somewhat by adding that the house is large and the color of it is controlled by a covenant community, that the lawn is free of both decoration and spare car parts, and that the car is actually a minivan or an SUV so that mom can drive the kids to soccer practice.

At best, the American Dream meant doing better than your parents had. It was reflected in the eyes of immigrants when they first saw the Statue of Liberty. They seemed to say, I might come to America with wooden shoes, but my children will do better than I am doing, and their children will do even better.

At worst, the American Dream has become rampant materialism. Success is measured by what you have, and work is for the purpose of buying more things. A certain bumper sticker sums it up well: "He who dies with the most toys wins." What's disturbing is the attitude of entitlement that has coat-tailed on the American Dream. No longer do I simply hope and work hard to do better than my parents; it is my right now to do better and to have more.

Further, the fact that I have more doesn't mean that I help out other people more.

> In 1933, the worst year of the Great Depression, per capita income was at the lowest point it would reach between 1921 and 2000, whether measured in current or inflation-adjusted dollars. Yet per member giving among the 11 primary Protestant denominations (or their historical antecedents) in the United States and Canada as a percentage of income was 3.3 percent. In all the prosperity of 2000, per member giving was only 2.6 percent.[8]

In other words, the mindset seems to be, let them pull themselves up by their own bootstraps. Poor people, homeless people, have brought it on themselves, so let them fix it themselves. George Barna, the pre-eminent pollster of religion in America, notes, "Most analysts would agree that 1999 was one of the best financial years we have experienced in a long time. If we experience declining generosity by Americans during a period of unusual financial favor, what should we expect when the economy hits a downturn?"ix The group with the lowest percentage of giving to either churches or non-profit organizations? Hispanics – our largest growing population.

Nothing in the history of the world has been promoted more effectively worldwide than the American Dream. It is our greatest export. Churches sent missionaries to Japan for years, and while we may or may not have taught the Japanese how to be good Christians, we certainly taught them how to become great Americans; and now Japan fulfills the American Dream by making better cars, better entertainment units, and better cell phones.

The American Dream as traditionally defined falls squarely at the Individualistic extreme of the model. Success is defined by independence, by the number and kind of degrees you have, by how self-reliant you are. The Individualistic extreme is a matter of power, and it's in our nature to fight to retain the power we have even as we, perhaps unwittingly, perhaps not, keep the powerless on the other side of the model.

So what will the American Dream look like in the New America, the America that is becoming brown? I am more and more convinced that the face of powerful/powerless isn't going to change so much as are the techniques of becoming powerful. White Americans, the traditional holders of the American Dream, became powerful through formal education, earned degrees, and white privilege. African Americans, Asian Americans, and Latinos are coming up through entrepreneurships and small businesses. For example, take the push-cart churros.

A "war" is being waged right now in California over churros, a dough that is strained through a star-tipped funnel, then fried in hot oil, and rolled in cinnamon sugar or sprinkled with powered sugar. Street vendors are allowed to sell frozen items but not hot items. What about hotdogs? Hotdogs are okay to sell because they are boiled right there, presumably destroying any disease-carrying bacteria. Churros are not. So churros are off-limits to street carts. The result of making the push-cart churros illegal – besides giving the public a greatly inferior product – is to limit entrepreneurship, the very thing the American Dream wants to encourage. The governor's desk has a bill on it waiting for his decision in this food war that reflects America's changing face.

That's the American Dream. So instead of becoming powerful through education, Latinos want to become powerful through entrepreneurship, through selling churros on the street. This has become a fight because Latinos are not participating in the American Dream through the standard means.

Rather than the New America being defined along racial lines by asking whether we are a melting pot or a salad bowl, I suggest we look deeper, particularly in light of the American Dream, and ask what side of the Individualistic/Enmeshed model we are on, no matter our color, our gender, or our religion. Ultimately, I think and hope to show shortly, race doesn't matter as long as I stay next to people who are like me on the model.

Take, for instance, the story of a friend's co-worker. Pat Gonzales had attended Denver Public Schools in the late sixties. He went all the way through with the same group of kids from the neighborhood – all white kids. One day, his close friend said to him, "I heard we're getting a 'greaser' in school." He was a little afraid, because he didn't know what a "greaser" was, but it didn't sound good. His mother told him that that was a bad name for someone from Mexico. He ganged up with the rest of his friends and wouldn't talk to the Mexican boy when he got there; after all, there's "us" and then there's "them," and the "greaser" was definitely not one of "us." Then one day the Mexican boy came up to him and said, "Hey, we've got to stick together."

Pat said, "What do you mean?"

"Well," he said, "we Mexicans have to stick together."

Until that time, Pat didn't have any idea that he was different, that he also wasn't one of "us."

Like the fish in water, we often don't recognize the culture we are in. It is as natural to us as the air we breathe. We don't recognize it until we try talking to someone on the "outside," someone who breathes a little different air or floats in a different lake.

The culture we've been in since the 1960s, and the war we have fought since then, has been one of racism, but I'm convinced that the problem isn't solely with race. It's with power. Before I discuss power, let me explain why we have focused on race as the problem.

## Racism

In the 1960s, many people, including the government officials, were concerned with civil rights. This tumultuous decade saw the rise of the Civil Rights Movement, the Civil Rights Act, the Congress of Racial Equality, and the birth of affirmative action. What was at issue in the struggles of those times was power. The powerless, traditionally blacks, were taking action in order to gain power. Affirmative action, instituted by President Lyndon Johnson in 1965, focused particularly on education and jobs.

> Affirmative action policies required that active measures be taken to ensure that blacks and other minorities enjoyed the same

opportunities for promotions, salary increases, career advancement, school admissions, scholarships, and financial aid that had been the nearly exclusive province of whites. From the outset, affirmative action was envisioned as a temporary remedy that would end once there was a "level playing field" for all Americans.[10]

The level playing field, however, never came about. The reason? The primary problem was not race but power.

Martin Luther King, Jr. believed the problem to be a spiritual one, and he believed that there were two options to deal with it. One was revolution in the streets, which the powerless would lose because the powerful would simply crush them. The other option was to call it sin and let God deal with it. He believed that if resistance was done in the power of the Holy Spirit, power could be brought to its knees. He was right, and his non-violent approach brought the system to its knees. The country, though, never saw it as a spiritual issue. Even the church missed him as the great spiritual leader of the time. Everyone saw King as a great social activist, but because he was a black man, the country saw what he was talking about as a racial issue.

We still say that race is the most contentious issue in the country. I don't think it is any more. I think power is. Getting people to see their own power struggles, though, is like pinning Jell-o to the wall. You hear some white people all the time saying, "I'm not a racist. Some of my best friends are black." That's because the issue isn't race. If you are powerful, can you say that some of your best friends are the powerless, no matter what their race?

It goes back to the American Dream. The backlash against affirmative action should have been foreseeable. "In a country that prized the values of self-reliance and pulling oneself up by one's bootstraps, conservatives resented the idea that some unqualified minorities were getting a free ride on the American system."[11] As noted earlier, we will fight to maintain the power we have. The American Dream is not about giving up power.

If our country prizes "self-reliance" and the "bootstrap theory," then it doesn't matter what color one is as long as one fits in with the American model. The human race has always viewed different as bad and as inferior. As Friedrich Nietzsche said, "The surest way to corrupt a youth is to instruct him to hold in higher esteem those who think alike than those who think differently." The Individualistic extreme of the model states, if you want to be successful, then you must become like me; become like me because my way is better. And as Nietzsche saw, that is the way of corruption. The problem isn't racism. The more I deal with relationships, the more I have come to realize that the issue that divides this country has very little to do with race. People in this country suffer from "differentism."

## Not Racism, but Differentism

If you take a white girl and a black girl and raise them together in the same neighborhood, same socio-economic status, they wouldn't see themselves as white against black. But put them together later, perhaps in their teenage years, with a Native American whom they've never seen before, and they'd be seen as racist. However, what it is is differentism. We're scared to death of being around people who are different.

In the early days of affirmative action, there were few people of color in corporations. I was one of the first, and they sent us out to recruit other Latinos, because businesses saw that things were changing, and they knew we had to bring in people. They really didn't care what color you were if you had the grades to become a CPA. If you made money for them, they didn't care. What did surprise them were the cultural differences. I recruited Manny Espinoza for Peat Marwick in 1975. He was a bright guy from Nogales, Arizona, and I convinced the firm to hire him. I still remember the first day he came to work. It was in July in Arizona. Because it was so hot, we were told we could wear our short-sleeve white shirts and ties, but we could forego the jackets. On Manny's first day, he showed up wearing white shoes and a lime green leisure suit. He looked perfect for going to the disco, but this was an accounting firm! My boss, as could have been predicted, called me into his office to find out what was up with the new guy. To some, it might have looked racist. But his skin color wasn't the problem.

It wasn't about race or looks or even differing values. It was the behaviors that many people weren't used to. A friend who used to do research and development for the University of Denver said, "White-collar people tend to shower in the morning. They're going to be in the office all day and want to be clean. Blue-collar people tend to shower at night. They've worked hard all day at manual labor and want to be clean. They value the same thing; only their behavior is different."

Affirmative action was supposed to be the equalizer. It was supposed to take the person of color and give her opportunities that she wouldn't have had a chance at before because of her color. And affirmative action did its job. However, what is affirmative action's job now? It cannot continue to be defined in the same way. For example, let's say that the University of Colorado at Boulder is considering two applications to attend school, one from a wealthy African-American woman from Denver and the other from a poor white man from the San Luis Valley. Traditional affirmative action would give it to the African-

American woman. Affirmative action, however, needs to re-evaluate. It still needs to function as an equalizer, but *what it needs to equalize is the powerful and the powerless.* That kind of affirmative action would give the poor white student from San Luis preference. I'm not sure America is ready to deal yet with that kind of shift in perspective. When we talk about power, we're hitting at the very heart of America. America is power. The American Dream is power. But we are more used to framing the issue in terms of race.

Because we fear those who are different, we tend to associate with those who are like us. It's a whole issue of mindset, or what some will call worldview, of where you were raised on that Individualistic/Enmeshed model. No one looks more different than the ones on the other side of that model.

Traditionally, white males have been on the Individualistic extreme, which was equated with power; people of color and women have been on the Enmeshed extreme, which was equated with powerlessness. Affirmative action has done its job, and now we find all colors and genders on both extremes of the model. The issue now is not the conflict between black and white or between male and female. The true issue is between those with power (whatever race or gender) and those without power (whatever race or gender).

In South Central Los Angeles, now known just as South L.A., traditional ways of dealing with challenges are no longer working. Once a largely African-American community, South L.A. is now predominantly Latino, and what worked before may not work again.

> The challenges in addressing the area's problems – regarding jobs, education and public safety – go beyond race and are now often spoken of in economic and social

terms rather than exclusively ethnic ones. Those who promote exclusively race-based approaches and resist the new ethnic dynamics no longer offer a working strategy for dealing with the problems of such communities.[12]

We know that some people are kept down; we know that there is a glass ceiling. However, most of the time, especially in the last twenty years, the problem is one of mindset. If you have the mindset of the CEO, you will tend to be on the Individualistic side. We tend to hire people who think like us. So the CEO will hire vice presidents and middle managers who are on the Individualistic extreme, regardless of race or gender. You will find women in those positions; you'll find people of color in those positions. What you won't find are people who don't hold to that Individualistic mindset or subscribe to those Individualistic values. Presidents of colleges will hire faculty members who hold to the same ideals. And again, it doesn't matter what race or gender they are. For instance, the administrators and board members of a seminary I'm affiliated with talks about being committed to diversity; they conducted a national search to fill a faculty position with a person of color and were thrilled when they appointed a black man. But if you look at that black man, he thinks like they do, went to the same predominantly white, conservative schools they did, lives in the same conservative (and white) neighborhood they do, and buys into the same theology they do. He has no idea what the black community is like. Neither do they. The only difference between him and them is skin color. That's not diversity, even if it looks more diverse statistically.

And that's the real issue.

# The Powerful and the Powerless

Racism is not the main issue, because today we're dealing with the powerful and the powerless. All genders, all races, every group. The Bible speaks to that issue. Jesus said, "The poor will be with you always," but it won't always be the same poor.

We import the poor. In World War II, America allowed immigrants into America through what was known as the "braceros" program. Braceros, from the Spanish word "brazos" for arms, defined people who did manual labor by picking fruit and building highways and railroads, and we brought in as many as we needed. It was an oppressive system that allowed employers to pay low wages if any at all, and to threaten deportation or jail to those who protested. We imported the poor; now we can't stop them from coming, and we don't know what to do about it. Now, because they've bought into the American Dream, they're oppressing the new group at the bottom.

In order to understand how the powerless move to the powerful – how Enmeshed moves to Individualistic – let's look at the stages of colonization.

Albert Memmi, the author of *The Colonizer and the Colonized*, writes that first, the colonizer (in this book, the Individualistic extreme) must rewrite the history of the colonized (the Enmeshed extreme). He uses the example of the French taking over Timbuktu, which used to be the New York City of Africa. The French redefined the people and did it so well that even today if you talk about someone going out into the sticks, into the far-off reaches of civilization, you talk about Timbuktu. The French had to redefine them from the outside. "They're illiterate (in other words, they don't speak French), therefore, they're savages." Once the colonizer redefines from the outside, the

48

colonized begin to redefine themselves that way. Colonization creates stereotypes, which adds to the illusion of racism, but is in fact differentism. To give an example of it in today's demographically shifting terms, "Latinos are lazy." If that were really true, why would white America want them to pick its fruit, clean its houses, and nanny its children?

That's what we're doing in Iraq. We have to redefine the Iraqis to the Americans in order to justify bombing them. In a recent interview, Saddam Hussein's daughters talked about their father in loving terms. They said how they knew that he loved them and would care for them and protect them. One of the reporters asked, "How do you deal with the fact that he killed both of your husbands?" One daughter said, "That was part of the protection." No one who has heard it from our side would believe that Saddam is capable of love or of care, because we're redefining who he is.

The next stage is the first response by the colonized. "Hell no. I'm not a lazy Mexican." If the colonizer keeps it up long enough, eventually the response will be, "Maybe, but not me." Maybe my people are that way, but I'm not. Perhaps I'm one of the ones who become successful (by becoming like you, of course). The colonizers then say, "See? You people are lazy, but look at Stan Perea – he became a CPA, so you can too." The few that make it would have made it no matter what. The colonizer, though, makes them an example to the colonized that they could do it, too, if only they would change, but they aren't willing to change. Some of the white backlash to affirmative action expresses this response. "Why could some minorities who had also experienced terrible adversity and racism—Jews and Asians, in particular—manage to make the American way work for them without government handouts?"[13]

The next response is "Yes, but this is better." So you might have the colonizer saying, "Mexicans are lazy, they're never on time," and we might agree. Latinos are not very tied to time. When you have a party in a Latino family, you say to come over "Whenever, 8:30, 9:00, whenever." So the response to the colonizer is, "Yes, we're always late, but we don't run our lives by a clock. We're not stressed. This is better."

The final response is "Hell no, we will define who we are." When this happens, all hell breaks loose, because the colonized are no longer colonized. What happens when they are no longer the colonized? They become the colonizer by accepting the standards the previous colonizers set.

Memmi notes:

> In order for the colonizer to be a complete master, it is not enough for him to be so in actual fact, but he must also believe in the [colonial system's] legitimacy. In order for that legitimacy to be complete, it is not enough for the colonized to be a slave, he must also accept his role. . . . One is disfigured into an oppressor, a partial, unpatriotic and treacherous being, worrying only about his privileges and their defense; the other into an oppressed creature, whose development is broken and who compromises by his defeat.[14]

The colonizer must believe in the system's legitimacy; in other words, the Individualistic extreme (largely Anglo) must buy into the American Dream. The colonized, the Enmeshed extreme (largely Latino), also buy into it by accepting the standards and definitions that the colonized have set. If the Enmeshed want a place at the trough, they must become Individualistic. If Latinos, Blacks, and Asians want a place at the trough, they must become White.

We always need the powerless; we always need somebody to step on. People become more conservative, on the Individualistic side, when they have more to conserve. If you don't have anything, you're much more likely to say, "Let's share everything." African Americans and Latinos used to fight for unemployment benefits; now that some of them have moved over to the more powerful side – the side of employers – they don't want to give out unemployment benefits. The Individualistic extreme strives to maintain the status quo, which means keeping power on the one hand and oppressing the powerless on the other.

The demographics are shifting and will therefore shift power. The power structure will look different, but we won't do away with the powerful/powerless structure itself. Once the Latinos change America, brown America will start bringing in Indonesians to clean the toilets. There's always going to be someone we bring in to do the dirty work no one else wants to do. The powerful are never going to clean toilets. Someone has to clean them – we'll hire or import people to clean them. People who fear immigration talk about immigrants taking jobs away from Americans. They're not taking jobs away. We're giving them away. We don't want them. A *New York Times* article states that 82 percent of Hispanics said that "immigrants take jobs that Americans do not want." Sylvia Gonzalez, a custodian who moved to Denver from Mexico, stated, "In Mexico, one can study and study, but there's no good work when you finish school. Here we do the jobs that no one wants to do because we know the value of work. Here we understand that the person without a job is the person who does not have the will to work."[15]

Karl Marx talked about the cycle of oppression. When the peasants or the underclass have enough of oppression, they will stage a peasant revolt and become the upperclass. Then the entire cycle starts again. That's what is happening now. The Latinos are staging a peasant revolt, except that instead of shooting them, we're marrying them! We marry them, and they become like us, and we become like them, and we become this new generation of people. But that new generation will someday become the oppressors.

Because Latinos have traditionally been on the Enmeshed side, success may be defined differently with the shifting demographics. Oppression will be different, but we'll still have it. We may be more gentle oppressors, but we'll still be oppressors. The only advance from the oppressive migrant working conditions of the sixties when we first started bringing the issue up is that migrant workers today have a little bit better housing. But they're still migrant workers and they still work twenty hours a day and they still bring in the fruit. Affirmative action made bosses out of some of the workers in the field, but they're not treating the ones who are still in the field any better than they were before. Nobody wants video cameras showing people in what kind of rat-holes these people live. It's not as though we're giving them pay raises every six months or better health care. So oppression may look different, we may soften the way oppression looks, but it will still be there.

## The Answer

As I stated earlier, affirmative action was meant to be the great equalizer. Another Great Depression would be an equalizer – everyone's equal when we're all "cleaning toilets." So much of the Individualistic/Enmeshed divide, though, is found in the human heart, and no amount of structural change or legislation or personal badgering will change that.

So, if we can't change the human heart, and can't

change the Individualistic/Enmeshed model, what hope is there? The gospel is the hope we're looking for. The gospel is about equalizing. From a spiritual standpoint, the Bible says in Romans that we're all sinners. We're all equal in that respect. We're all in need of a Savior. Despite what many evangelicals think, though, there is more than just this spiritual side of us. God is very concerned with social injustice. Most of the Old Testament prophecies call judgment down on those who mistreat the powerless. Micah 6:8 asks the question, "What does the LORD require of you?" It answers it with a phenomenal blend of physical and spiritual aspects. "To act justly and to love mercy and to walk humbly with your God." How we treat the poor or the powerless is how we're going to be judged.

The church is the body that is called to deal with the issue of power. The church, however, doesn't have a very good track record; it operates under the same Individualistic/ Enmeshed model. This will be looked at in detail in Chapter 9. The powerful/powerless structure has become a success, and it has moved into the church. The church looks at success the same way the world does. Success in the church is defined, thanks in part to the church growth movement, by how many people you bring in the door, how beautiful your building is, how much you spend on ministry. It certainly isn't defined by how poor you are.

The church has finally started to deal with the issue of race, and some think that it's still not doing a good job there. At least we have reached the point where we'll call racism sin. But we haven't yet called power sin. We go to great lengths to tell people that they're not greedy, that there's nothing wrong with how much they have. Very few people are out there trying to get poorer or trying to give up power, and yet that's what the gospel is about. Jesus said, "If anyone wishes to come after me, let him deny himself, take up his cross, and follow me." But that's un-American. That's not the American Dream.

Although the gospel is about pouring yourself out for others, about not grasping power, Christians are talking one game while playing another. They are trying to live in both worlds. Bill Hybels, of Willow Creek Community Church in South Barrington, IL, wrote about living in two worlds. He compared Janis Joplin, Mother Teresa, and Princess Diana. Janis Joplin believed that sex, drugs, and rock and roll would bring her happiness. She poured her life into that, and she died living that lifestyle. Mother Teresa believed that giving up personal power and pouring herself into the service to others would bring her happiness. She also died living the lifestyle in which she believed. Princess Diana tried to live in both worlds. She was known for her philanthropy and many people mourned her death because of how good she was. But she was also known for a fast lifestyle that included drugs and materialism. Ultimately, she couldn't live in both worlds.

We can't live in both worlds either. When God calls us to take care of the powerless, he expects us to take that command as seriously as we take the commands about adultery. The powerless are not only those found in wombs.

## Notes

[1] Joel Kotkin, and Thomas Tseng, "Happy to Mix It All Up," *Washington Post*, June 8, 2003.

[2] Maria Puente and Martin Kasindorf, "Blended Races Making a True Melting Pot," *USA Today*, Sep 7, 1999, 13A.

[3] Maria Puente and Martin Kasindorf, 15A.

[4] David Brooks, "People Like Us," *The Atlantic Monthly*, Sep 2003: 29.

[5] David Brooks, 30.

[6] Haya El Nasser, "Hispanic Growth Reveals Isolation," *USA Today*, Mar 26, 2001.

[7] Sharon Noguchi, "Separate, Equal and Dangerous," *Mercury News*, 1999.

[8] John L. and Sylvia Ronsvalle, *The State of Church Giving through 2000* (Champaign, IL: Empty Tomb, 2002), p. 33.

[9] http://www.barna.org/cgi-bin/PagePressRelease.asp?PressReleaseID=52&Reference=B

[10] Borgna Brunner, "Bakke and Beyond: A History and Timeline of Affirmative Action," http://www.infoplease.com/spot/affirmative1.html.

[11] Borgna Brunner. Of course part of the answer to this question is that Jews, Asians, and Hispanics haven't had to deal with decades of slavery. While each of these groups has had oppression to deal with, none has been so harsh or so hard to overcome as the oppression of African and Native Americans.

[12] Joel Kotkin, and Thomas Tseng. Emphasis mine.

[13] Borgna Brunner.

[14] Albert Memmi, *Colonizer and Colonized* (Boston: Beacon Press, 1965), 89.

[15] Simon Romero and Janet Elder, "Hispanics More Optimistic than Other U.S. Groups," *The New York Times*, Aug. 10, 2000.

# Chapter 3
## The Idol of the Family

No matter what issue we're discussing, whether it's politics or health care or education or television, the family is affected by all of them. We heard enough about "family values" in the 1996 and 2000 election campaigns to confuse us. If Hillary Clinton and George W. Bush are both tossing the term around, it can't mean the same thing, can it? "Family values" is basically trying to define what family is. The problem is that everyone is fighting so much over the definition that little is getting done to help the situation. In this chapter, then, we'll discuss how the Individualistic and Enmeshed extremes look at family and some of the issues facing the family.

## The Family as Idol

While family is an important institution, one that many Christians believe started when God said "Adam, meet Eve, now go and procreate," we've seen in the last ten years an elevation of the family. Or make that, The Family.

The church has been one of the great proponents of the family, and has gone to great lengths to protect it from the influences that it sees as threatening, particularly from the gay community. Before we can define the threat, let's look at what some people are trying to protect.

Say the word "family" and most people in America get the picture of husband, wife, 2.5 kids and a dog. The house will be in suburbia, have a two-car garage, and one of the cars – Mom's car, most likely – will have a bumper sticker about an honor roll student. Dad works in a white-collar job, and Mom stays home.

How does this image square with what we experience in America? Not well. Married couples made up nearly 80 percent of the households in the 1950s; today that number is 50.7 percent. Over 30 percent of children live with a single parent. Of that 30 percent, approximately 9 percent who live with their mothers also live with the mothers' cohabiting partner. In 2000, 66 percent of children had two working parents (or one, if they lived with a single parent). Of children from birth to third grade (approximately the first nine years of their lives), 54 percent receive some form of childcare.

These kinds of statistics usually lead to hand wringing and the cry, similar to Helen Lovejoy's on "The Simpsons," "Won't someone please think of the children." People, and those in the church in particular, have a knee-jerk reaction and are sure that the country is going to hell in a handbasket. What we need, they often say, is a return to the days when "family" meant "family." Let's go back to the 1950s when God sanctioned what the family was to be. Family values then become a way of telling people how they should behave and what families should look like.

The problem is, we're never going to return to the 1950s! And if we define family as "husband, wife, and 2.5 kids," as we did in the 1950s, we're disenfranchising a lot of families. It is not fair to describe families as "broken" if they don't look the way they looked in the 1950s. If we look at family the way Focus on the Family looks at family, then we have Jesus coming out of a broken family. We have Timothy coming out of a broken family. We've made an idol out of the family. This idolatry assumes that if you're not part of an intact family, you're not anything.

The church has always had trouble ministering to singles. We just don't know what to do with them. So, a lot of singles ministries resemble nightclubs without the alcohol, a kind of dating service with prayer thrown in for good measure. Let's get the singles married as soon as possible so that they can join the real church ministry.

And it's not just singles. Try being married with no children in church. If you're young, you're okay, because you just haven't started your real family. What about if you can't have children? You might get pity, but little else. What if you and your spouse have decided for whatever reason not to have children? Then there is something wrong with you. As a friend said to me, the unspoken 11th commandment in the church is "Have children."

# Children According to the Extremes

## The Individualistic Extreme

So, what do we do with children when we have them? On the Individualistic extreme, we have children to reflect our success, and we raise them to be successful, to achieve the American Dream. We hear a lot of preaching and a lot of messages and policy making about the irresponsibility of kids today, and how kids need to be more responsible like we were when we were kids. This line of thinking astounds me. When I was in junior high, you were doing well and being responsible if you went the entire week without forgetting your lunch. It was "Ozzie and Harriet" and

"Leave It to Beaver." Harriet or June made your lunch – and this after making sure that you had a hot, nutritious breakfast – met you at the door, gave it to you on the way out and kissed you good-bye while telling you to "be a good boy." Many of the kids today have to fix their own breakfast, take care of their brother or sister before they go to school, maybe feed them breakfast, make sure everyone has their lunch money, and lock up the house when they leave. Then we say, "They're irresponsible. They should be more responsible like we were when we were kids." There is a push, then, for family to be what we would like it to be or what we thought it was for us.

It doesn't matter that those shows were on television forty years ago; the dream of what they represented still holds. The dream, though, for Ward and June Cleaver, parents of the Beaver, mainly involved keeping the Beaver out of trouble; nothing serious, like drugs or gangs or school shootings, just regular "boys-will-be-boys" trouble. But the innocence of "Leave It to Beaver" is gone. The innocence has given way to the push to be successful. It's not enough any more for the parent to be successful at his or her job. In order to find the American Dream, the children must now be successful as well, in school and out. David Goetz puts it well:

> It seems that every child in the more affluent suburbs is tag—talented and gifted. The environmental pressures to nurture children toward success tend to bloat one's life: park district soccer, tee-ball, swimming. Then the traveling leagues, clubs, drama, youth group outings. Finally special classes or tutors to prepare for the SAT. The covert pressure is to move upward in housing, friends, "educational opportunities" (for example,

spring break family trips to Paris), and vacations.[1]

In order to be deemed successful, parents raise children to leave home at eighteen, go to college, graduate college, get a "good" job, and start their own families. One thing that we're wrestling with right now is that many kids are coming back home. They go to college and then return. Sometimes, particularly now in tough economic times, there isn't a job waiting for them. This also is part of the problem with the American Dream. Parents have raised their children to expect what they call "good" jobs, meaning jobs that pay well. We've lost respect for someone who is a hard worker at a job that is considered menial. A good job means a white-collar job. So, the kids graduate from college, can't get jobs that pay $40,000 entry level, and then move back in with Mom and Dad. And a lot of parents are distressed about that. They're coming into counseling offices, including mine, and asking, "What did we do wrong?" There's a sense that we've failed to get these kids out of the house and on their own.

## The Enmeshed Extreme

At the Enmeshed extreme, you never leave the family, and whoever lives with you is considered family. At the Enmeshed extreme, there is no such thing as a broken family. Family is family no matter what it looks like.

A growing phenomenon in the immigrant population is that of common law marriage. As a pastor, I have to deal with that issue a lot, but it's an issue with which the church as a whole struggles. I have people who have been in the church for two or three years, who then come and tell me that they've never been married. But family is family. Are they living in sin?

You have kids that are being raised by Grandma and Grandpa in communal families. Is that considered a broken family? You have a 42-year-old brother and a 37-year-old sister and a 70-year-old mom living together. Is that dysfunctional?

If it's built on relationships, it doesn't matter. In my view, there's no such thing as a broken family, because if you're dealing with a brother, sister, and mom and they're all adults, that's a family. The Individualistic extreme sees that as fairly dysfunctional.

When I was growing up, it wasn't uncommon to have Hispanics put in classes for the mentally retarded, because we didn't know how many people were in our family. We would go to school, and the teacher would ask, "How many people are in your family?" "Eleven." "Eleven? Are you sure?" "Yes." Then the next week, maybe we're asked the same question. "How many people are in your family?" This time, we might say, "Fifteen," because our aunt and uncle and their two kids moved in with us, and they're part of family. Whoever was living with us at the time was counted as family. They weren't treated differently from the rest of the family. It seemed simple, but the school system didn't understand that. Their thinking was that by the time you're in the fourth grade, you should know how many people are in your family.

Times, though, are changing as the once-immigrant population learns the system and buys into the American Dream. Immigrant families are still having a large number of kids; they're still coming here thinking that more kids will earn more money and that the family can then have a better life. It takes them a generation or two to realize that that's not the way it works here.

Let's look at family planning for a moment. On the Individualistic extreme, we plan carefully how many children we will have, how many we can take care of. The more kids you have, the less you can provide for them. Remember, providing for them on the Individualistic extreme means more than providing shelter and food and maybe health insurance. Providing also means safe transportation (the SUV), soccer practices, piano lessons, and private schools at times because the public schools don't do their job. In a place that's driven by me-ism, we can't have too many children and still afford the same lifestyle.

So then, we say to immigrants, you have too many children; you can't provide for them. The other extreme, though, is somewhat fatalistic. Their answer is, "Sea la voluntad de Dios." "It is the will of God." So if someone were sick and dying, it was difficult and people were sad, but "may it be the will of God." We didn't have the bootstrap theory that said, "I'll work hard, and I'll take care of this." It was, "the will of God." In this success driven, Individualistic model, to simply accept "the will of God" is a cop-out, it is failure. Yet to Latinos, that was a driving force.

Part of the issue with large numbers of children is religious. The majority of Mexicans are Roman Catholic, and the Catholic Church teaches that to use any kind of contraceptive is to go against the will of God. The biblical model taught that children were a blessing of God; therefore, the more children the better. It proved God's blessing upon your family and proved that you trusted God for the wealth to provide. However, while some of this issue is religious, it is also cultural. There is a certain machismo to having a large family. It's manly, it's fiesta, to rural cultures it's help on the farm.

The Individualist extreme, of course, doesn't believe that "it is the will of God." You can determine your own will. If you can't afford that many children, don't have them. It's irresponsible. And it compounds the

irresponsibility to believe that the government should
help out.

In *Mexifornia*, Victor Davis Hansen talks about the way
in which the public school system educated Hispanics, and
I remember it being the way he describes in Antonito. We
sang "America the Beautiful" and learned the Pledge of
Allegiance. We learned how to speak English and were
taught American history and civics. We learned that white
was right, and that even Mexicans could be like white
people if we worked hard enough. We learned that Jesus
was blond. I sat through classes and thought, "Why don't
Mexicans have any heroes? How come the Mexicans never
did anything?" While the Hispanics and the Americans
were learning the same things in those classrooms, it wasn't
generating the same kind of ownership and feelings. We
learned that if we wanted to fit in, we had to limit the
number of kids we had in order to give them what we didn't
have growing up. And now, because we have bought into
the American Dream, second and third generation Hispanic
families are having less children because we want to be able
to give them all we can. But in an effort to give them what
we didn't have, we have failed to give them what we did
have. We give them $120 sneakers, cellphones, television
sets, CD players. But we have neglected to give them our
time, or to see that our families have meals together or
watch television together. We do not teach our children to
learn to do without or to at least wait until some money has
been saved, and they never learn to share or realize that
sometimes everyone can't have their own stereo or
television.

The birth rate is declining in other communities as well.
In fact, the Centers for Disease Control and Prevention
released figures in June 2003 that show that the United
States has reached a record low in the birth rate, 1 percent
lower than in 2001 and a whopping 17 percent lower than

in 1990. In fact, while the trend used to be an average of 2.5 children per couple, today's trend is 1.8 and falling. While celebrating the fact that teen birth rates are down, some concern is voiced over the decline for women in their prime child-bearing years. Many women are waiting to have children and are, therefore, having fewer children. And with many people believing that more children means that everyone gets less, there are more single-child families than there ever have been, with approximately 20 percent of families having an "only child."

Another way that the American Dream has hurt immigrant families is in the area of abortion. Teenage pregnancies have always been a part of history. In the Hispanic population, children of teenaged mothers just grew up with the rest of the family. Family is family, remember? But now with Mom and Dad chasing the American Dream, both working, no one at home, it's become a major issue. The powerful idea that we want our kids to get out of the house and go to college in order to become a productive member of society means that we procure abortions for our daughters.

Family issues also deal with blended families. His kids, her kids, and their kids. I'm one of ten kids, and when I think of the fighting we did in our family – all from the same set of parents – I can't imagine what it would be like to have a blended family. And if it's difficult for the siblings, it's not any easier for the parents. In a study done for Sex Roles, researchers found that having more children is associated with better health for women. However, "women with stepchildren in their homes have significantly worse physical and mental health than women without stepchildren. Being remarried, in contrast with being married, is not beneficial for women's health."[2]

# Single Mothers: The New Poor

We can't talk about non-traditional families without talking about single mothers. Thirty percent of all children live with a single parent, in most cases (about 27 percent) with a mother. Right now, the highest poverty rate is among single moms and their kids, primarily due to what Michelle Conlin calls the "marriage-centric structure" of most businesses that give healthcare, retirement, and other benefits to married people. "'Most workplaces are still modeled on an outdated definition of an ideal worker – someone who works more than 50 hours a week and doesn't take breaks to raise children,' says Joan Williams, co-director of the Gender, Work & Family Project at the American University Law School. 'God forbid if you are [a] single mother trying to live up to that ideal without a wife.'"[3]

Children of single-parent homes have a hard future in front of them. They tend to do poorer in school, they don't have health insurance, suicide rates are higher, some of them worry about getting enough to eat. Marriage Savers, a national counseling ministry, offers these statistics: "Children of divorce or children of never-married parents are twice as likely to drop out of school; they're three times as likely to get pregnant themselves as teenagers, 12 times as likely to be incarcerated if they're children of divorce, 22 times more likely to be incarcerated if they're children of never-married parents."[4]

The statistics for out-of-wedlock births is alarmingly high, and it's not all teenagers. In fact, teen pregnancy is down. However, the rate for single women is climbing. In 1940, only 3.8 percent births were to unmarried women. Currently, the rate is 33 percent nationwide. In some areas, such as Baltimore, the figure is as high as 77 percent.

Baltimore also ranks among the ten large cities with the lowest median household income.

When we look at the statistics, single moms are the ones who are hurting the most. Look at how difficult it is for two parents to have jobs and still have time for their children! For one person to do it is pretty amazing. And overwhelming. And yet the American values, the Individualistic extreme has said that we need to get them off welfare and get them to work, get them into minimum wage jobs where there is no future. And by the way, let's eliminate childcare. Let's not offer flex time jobs or corporate sponsored day cares, because that cuts into a business' profits.

We need to set policies for the things that would help single moms. Think job sharing. Think affordable health insurance. Consider even the size of homes. Currently, we build homes for what we think of as families: three bedrooms, large den, family room, two-car garage. How many single moms need or can afford that? Our response is to say, "Let's build affordable housing." Yes, absolutely! But what do we do? We build *cheap* three bedroom homes with large dens, family rooms, and two-car garages. We use cheap materials that have been bought in the worst part of town, and then we build in the worst parts of town, but we still build the same kind of house. There's a need for us to begin to ask, "Do we need this?" Does it have to look like that or be that size?

Some people aren't convinced that President Bush's "pro-marriage" bill will help. (Isn't it ironic that today, some of the people who are most pro-marriage – the gays – are the ones we won't let get married?) In the bill, over $1 billion could be used over five years to promote marriage through advertising the benefits of marriage, offering premarital counseling services, and giving instruction in high schools. However, as Alexandra Starr notes, the new policy doesn't address the broader issues that many poor families face. "As Rachel Gragg, a social policy expert at the Center for Community Change, a liberal advocacy group, puts it: 'It's hard to devote yourself to a relationship when you're worried about whether you can buy food, pay the rent, and keep your kids safe.'"[5]

The debates over the Family Medical Leave Act exemplifies the extremes about family. The FMLA was passed by Congress in 1993. It addressed perceived stereotypes held by many employers who believed that if a family emergency required leave from work, it would be women rather than men who would take it. The FMLA states that all employees, men and women, are entitled to a total of up to twelve work weeks of unpaid leave during the year for the birth of a child, the care of a sick child or spouse, or a serious health condition of the employee. It aimed to take family emergency leave out of the realm of "women's issues" and place it as a gender-neutral employment benefit. It guarantees that an employee's job will be waiting when he or she gets back. As could be expected, many on the Individualistic extreme argued against the act, saying that it was going to drive business broke and that the government doesn't need to be involved in the running of businesses. The Enmeshed extreme is arguing that it isn't enough government involvement. Unpaid leave is worthless for people who are stretching to make ends meet.

It's the same argument with health care for children. It's not at all the case that the Individualistic extreme is cold and uncaring about sick kids. But people with this view look at the issue and say, "We've got to be practical. How can we get the private sector to handle that? How do we get the market to handle it, rather than have more government involvement?" The problem is, as we've seen before, the market won't handle it. There is no money in serving the poor. It's not going to happen. The Enmeshed extreme, on the other hand, says, "Let's let the government do it then," and the other side says, "Well, that means increased taxes and I don't want that." Both sides want to do it, but they have different ways of doing it. In the battle to do it "my way," we're not doing it. The poor are getting poorer while the two extremes argue. Both sides are genuinely concerned, but they have different approaches, and neither wants to compromise. And in arguing about the approach, nothing gets done.

The fact is we do have kids out of single parent homes struggling with life. We do have children who are sick and their parents don't have insurance. As long as we have these two extremes setting policy on the family, we're going to fight over a lot of things, and we're never going to deal with what family really is. We're going to deal instead with what we would like family to be.

I think that's what part of the problem with single moms is. We tend to punish those people who have strayed away from the cultural norm. Single moms have done that. In a purportedly Christian nation, we have very little compassion for those who are down-and-out, including single moms. Yet we study the scriptures about taking care of widows and orphans and the poor. If the scriptures hold true that we'll be judged by how we treat "the least of them," I think America is in for some horrendous judgment.

## On the Street Where You Live

How each side defines family is different. We've seen that. How each side decides what community to live in is different as well. On the Individualistic extreme, where we live is based on the services that are important to us. If I move to Lakewood, Colorado, it's because I like the school system or my church is there. Or, if I need a job, I pick up a newspaper and begin a job hunt. Maybe I'll call an employment agency. When I find a job, I look for a neighborhood that's close to my job, if possible. It's the services that draw me.

With the Enmeshed, it's relationships that draw me. Rather than finding a place to live that's close to a job, people at this extreme find a job that's close to the family. The Enmeshed extreme has a very powerful network, and that network will find work faster for their people than the Individualistic person will find one in the newspaper.

In the last two weeks, I've had nine people from Mexico and from Central and South America come into my office for help in finding work. One man, a twenty-two year old, is living with his sister who came from Mexico eight months ago. Her husband died of cancer in Mexico about four years ago, and she's here with her little girl and boy. They live in an apartment complex with 280 people. Of those, probably half have jobs somewhere. And because family is family, this twenty-two-year-old young man has approximately 140 people looking for a job for him. They look at their own places of employment. That's a powerful network.

This young man showed me his Social Security card and his Resident Alien card. I've seen several now in the last two weeks. They all look exactly alike, so I asked where he got them. He bought them at the apartments. It's the first part of the process, he said. You get here, and the people who are already here teach you the ropes. You're going to need a Social Security card and a Resident Alien card, they said. There's a van that comes by once a week to take your picture, so wear a nice shirt. Someone brings out a screen, takes your picture, and gives you your cards. It costs $160. I've seen nine in the last two weeks; at $160 a piece, that's a nice bit of change – that's entrepreneurship at its best!

So the people at these apartment complexes will help the immigrant get set up. The people living in these small apartments are all from the same part of Mexico. So people are moving around to different apartments, finding the community they belong in. If you lived in Matamoros, Mexico, you move around until you find the apartment for the people from Matamoros, Mexico. It's like "my home town" then – it just moved from there to here. The immigrant may move into the wrong apartment complex at first, but after a while the people there will say, "Oh, a lot of the people from your part of Mexico live over there." You'll meet them and party with them, then they will help you find work, and they will let you know when an apartment is vacant so you can move in. For the Enmeshed, breaking away is almost impossible. Part of this is that effort to make sure that we don't have someone from our neighborhood living "over there." They're part of us, so we've got to have them over here. As soon as an apartment opens up, we'll call you. Let's get him a job over here, so he can work with "our people," not with "those people."

A Mexican woman who is in the country illegally came into my office. She was brought by a *coyote*, the man who bought her a passport and charges money to get illegals here. This woman is staying in a home owned by relatives of the *coyote*. It doesn't matter that she doesn't know them. In the New America, you go to their house and now it's your house as well. When you come across the border, you don't have anything except the clothes on your back. In this woman's case, her relatives put her up, gave her clothes, and helped her find work in order to pay back the money spent to get her here and to get an apartment. She told me, "I can get two or three jobs, I can make it. I only need four or five hours of sleep." That's how strong the American Dream is. And how pathological it is. Three years from now, she'll be driving a nice car or pick-up truck and still working two or three jobs, still making minimum wage at each workplace, living in a place with two or three or five other Mexicans that she didn't know before, but now they're family. That is the new *familia* in this country.

# Our Aging Parents

Another important issue in talking about the family is that of our aging parents. Currently, there are approximately 35 million people aged 65 or older in the United States, which accounts for almost 13 percent of the total population. In 2011, the "baby boom" generation will begin to turn 65, and by 2030, it is projected that 70 million people, one in five people, will be age 65 or older. This means that within the next 30 years, programs and services will need to be developed to meet the demands of this larger-than-ever demographic.

According to the government's "Key Indicators of Well-Being" for older Americans, those who live alone are more likely to live in poverty, especially women. Approximately 41 percent of older white and older black women live alone, compared to 27 percent of Hispanic, Asian, and Pacific Islander women. Fifteen percent of white women live with other relatives, compared to almost 33 percent of black, Hispanic, Asian, and Pacific Islander women.

Many of the kids of my generation grew up with Grandma or Grandpa living with us. We learned from them and respected them. I'm now seeing in a lot of counseling situations siblings who are fighting over what to do with Mom and Dad. It used to be that the oldest was the next in line to be in charge of the family, so the oldest sibling would take Mom and Dad into his home. It didn't matter whether or not the oldest sibling had the ability or desire. Because he was the oldest, he was the one responsible for making the nest. Now, the oldest child brings Mom home to live with him, because he doesn't want Mom living alone. But that oldest boy and his wife are both working, and Mom is still living alone because the kids don't have time for her. So, he realizes that maybe Mom would be better off in a home with people there to take care of her.

Then the next oldest child goes to the home to visit Mom and says, "I'm not leaving my mother here," and she takes her to her home. And then it starts all over again. So we have these elderly people being bounced all around, and every time they bounce back and forth, it creates more problems in the family. Soon there is conflict in the entire family.

This reflects part of the Individualistic extreme. Turn Mom and Dad over to the specialists because they know how to deal with it. Soon, though, there will be more elderly than we know what to do with, and there won't be enough resources (people or money) to care for people the way we try to do now.

Once again, the immigrants are doing jobs that no one else wants to do. That's why there are so many immigrants working in nursing homes, taking care of our elderly. The Enmeshed extreme is moving in big ways into medical care and care of the aged. That will become one of the fastest growing industries in this country because of the aging of the baby boomers.

I'm going to give away an idea now that might help someone reading this to become a millionaire. If I were in the business world today, I would be investing in senior centers and nursing homes. I would set up a senior home that had mono-cultural pods that would exit to the courtyard. So, the home would have a Jewish wing, a Hispanic wing, an African-American wing, and so forth.

Elderly people still speak the languages and live in the cultures of the past. They don't want to go to a nursing home where they don't like the food or entertainment, where the others don't speak the same language. However, if they were put in places where they could spend time reminiscing with people of their own backgrounds, one could have a phenomenal business. Further, each pod could have its own type of worship service and entertainment.

Many of these populations have strong family ties. So here's how to lower costs. If someone wants to bring their parents there, then the family (the children and grandchildren) would volunteer time working at the senior home. If each extended family gave twenty hours per week, several needs would be met. First, a lot of the upkeep cost would be eliminated by having volunteers do the sweeping, washing windows, washing dishes, vacuuming, lawn care, and so forth. Second, the parents (or grandparents) would love to see their family around the place. If they knew that their families would be around on a regular basis, it would cut down on stress. Third, because the families would be volunteering to a non-profit organization, deductions could be taken for gas mileage. Finally, this volunteer program would benefit the grandchildren, who could stop in and have lunch with Grandma whenever they wanted. This could only strengthen the youth of our country.

Pearl S. Buck saw the need for familia and the need that the Individualistic extreme needs for community. She wrote, "The lack of emotional security of our American young people is due, I believe, to their isolation from the larger family unit. No two people - no mere father and mother - as I have often said, are enough to provide emotional security for a child. He needs to feel himself one in a world of kinfolk, persons of variety in age and temperament, and yet allied to himself by an indissoluble bond which he cannot break if he could, for nature has welded him into it before he was born."

# The Family's Bogey Man

We can't leave the issue of family without discussing something that a great many people think threatens the family and indeed the institution of marriage itself. The issue of family is a good fundraiser in this country. "Family values" is a good mantra that everyone wants to use to get money, to get votes. It becomes important, then, to define an enemy to fight, a bogey man to banish. We see the issues come and go like the tides of the ocean. Violence on television. Violence in the movies. Parental ratings on CDs. The school system (which we'll look at in the next chapter). The latest bogey man is gay marriage.

Gay marriage is a fight, I believe, over terms and what we want to protect. As I've said before, Hispanics can be rather schizophrenic when people try to label them. If the debate stays with the terms "gay marriage," then I think Hispanics will be opposed to it. But if we can move to terms such as "gay family," it will be different. Some people intentionally use the terms "marriage" because they know that people will react to it.

The fact is, the civil understanding of marriage is a contract between two people. It establishes certain rights regarding property, health coverage, death benefits, and taxes. A civil union between two people does not, indeed cannot, threaten the institution of marriage.

Most people, I think, are closer to the center than they are to the extremes on this issue. Extremists, though, carry the debate. Most people don't strongly care about these kinds of issues one way or the other until they are personally affected by them. For the majority of people, public education has been tolerable. Most people in this country move into a community and look for where the schools are. Most of them don't question, "Are there gay teachers here?" The reason the arguments are getting further out to the extremes is that the extremes are getting louder. The two political parties for all practical purposes are a thing of the past – it's only a matter of time before they collapse. They're looking at issues very differently, but the fact of the matter is that neither side gets anything done. So you have to start fighting about things to stay in the game – you have to make noise, so you become an extremist. For most people, gay marriage is not a big issue. But for the extremes, it's a hot issue, and it's an issue that raises money. Very often, the people, such as religious conservatives, who criticize gays for not being monogamous are the ones who fight the hardest against civil unions for gays. The questions we need to be asking are, do gay unions decrease promiscuity, is it just to deny medical rights to gay couples, why should the surviving partner of a gay union not receive death benefits?

Further, if we're going to criticize gays for their promiscuity, then it's time we criticize ourselves for the same thing. Is the threat to the family the homosexual couple next door, or is it really the faithlessness in our own heterosexual marriages?

One of the saddest things for us in Colorado right now is that Governor Bill Owens' 28-year marriage is falling apart. Bill and Frances Owens have been speaking on "family values" and the value of marriage for years. Mike Littwin, a columnist for the *Rocky Mountain News*, notes the irony of Colorado's first couple separating. Gov. Owens had promoted (and later dropped) the "Dr. Laura Bill," which would have mandated a year's worth of counseling to couples considering a divorce. "And now that Owens is going through the pain of this himself, I wonder if he might have second thoughts about the prospect of bringing the government, or Dr. Laura, into his private world."[6] Owens also signed the "Defense of Marriage Act" a few years ago that banned gay marriages. Littwin brings up an interesting point:

> In a country with too many divorces and with too many children born out of wedlock, it is surprising that somehow the pressing family issue seems to have become whether gays should be allowed to marry. As in the Owens' separation, this would seem, again, to be a private matter. And yet you get the "Defense of Marriage Act" Musgrave championed in the legislature and which Owens signed a few years ago . . . . Now Musgrave is a congresswoman and co-sponsor of a similar amendment to the U.S. Constitution that she says would protect the sanctity of marriage. Does she really think the foundation upon which, say, the Owens' marriage rests is threatened by the actions of some gay couple looking for the same legal protections that marriage confers upon the rest of the population?[7]

The issue here is not gay marriage. It is our own faithlessness, and being faithful is more than just saying no to the opposite sex if you're married.

Another issue that needs to be examined is the issue of adoption. We fight to bar gay couples from adopting children, and yet there are many children in this world who need loving parents. We try to talk women out of abortions by appealing to couples waiting to adopt – what if the adopting couple was gay? The sanctimonious preacher's wife Helen Lovejoy of "The Simpsons" has a favorite phrase: "Won't someone please think about the children?" If we in the church are all about the children, then why shouldn't we allow it? Can we put aside our own prejudices, and power issues, long enough to ask if a child might be better off with a loving gay couple than with a string of foster homes?

The perceived bogey man in the family issue is gay marriage. According to the Individualistic extreme, schools are out to indoctrinate and to convince our kids that homosexuality is right. They talk about the "gay agenda" without ever questioning their own agenda – and everybody has an agenda. We can't talk today about family without talking about gays. They are perceived as everything that is threatening the family. However, the family is being threatened by something much more pervasive and much more insidious.

## The Real Bogey Man

While extremists run around trying to convince us of the impending doom that gays are bringing upon the family, the true bogey man is running loose and creating havoc. The family in America is being threatened by something much more fundamental to our way of life than homosexuality, and that is the American Dream. Greed is destroying our families.

Currently running on television is a commercial for The Men's Wearhouse that signifies our obsession with success.[8] In this commercial, George Zimmerman, the owner, talks about the benefits of owning a great suit. He says that a great suit will help you get a better job, make more money, send the kids to better colleges so they'll make more money and buy you a retirement home on an island. That's the dream. That's success. Well, what if you don't have a suit? What if you're in a job that doesn't demand you wear a suit – not because it's Casual Friday, but because you're a laborer? Then you're not successful and you damn well better work harder.

The fact is, we are working harder. We've become workaholics in an effort to become "successful." From the 1970s to the 1990s, Americans added one month per year to their workload. Since it didn't come from a magical genie, where did the time come from? Well, Saturdays were the first to go. Next to go was sleep; Americans are sleeping less, almost two hours less a night. The average lunch "hour" is thirty-seven minutes. Obesity is a major problem in America, but where else can you eat in thirty-seven minutes other than the drive-through window at the fat-packed fast food place?

Mort Zuckerman wrote that Europeans work less hours and have more vacation time than Americans. It is government mandated. Zuckerman notes, "European labor unions push for more time off while American unions push for more money. We value more money and more stuff; they value more leisure time."[9]

So "family values" translates to "more money and more stuff." A recent article in the *New York Times* documented the rise in the use of credit cards, and not all of it is for frivolous things, but for everyday items that have skyrocketed in cost. The report, titled "Borrowing to Make Ends Meet," said:

> Between 1989 and 2001, credit card debt in America almost tripled, from $238 billion to $692 billion. The savings rate steadily declined, and the number of people filing for bankruptcy jumped 125 percent. . . . In the period studied, the credit card debt of the average family increased by 53 percent. For middle-class families, the increase was 75 percent. For senior citizens, 149 percent.

And for very low income families, with annual incomes below $10,000, the increase was a staggering 184 percent.[10]

A husband and wife have no time any more with each other or with the kids because they're both working, trying to maintain the lifestyle – the more money and more stuff – that the Individualistic extreme has deemed "successful." That is the bogey man. And if we want something that will help make our children better, stronger, less susceptible to the images they see on television and hear on the radio, then it is this bogey man that needs eradication.

## Redefining the Family

If we look at the scriptures, families don't look that much different today than they did then. There was a certain understanding of people. Jesus brought a message that said that those whom you consider unclean or off the wall or that don't fit the mold, that's who the kingdom of God is about. Jesus then said, "Who are my mother and my brothers and sisters?" He redefined the family and said that we are all adopted into his family. That's what family is. Richard Bach wrote, "The bond that links your true family is not one of blood, but of respect and joy in each other's life. Rarely do members of one family grow up under the same roof."

We might think that the "it takes a village to raise a child" mentality arose with the Clintons. It didn't. Jesus started it, and it can continue in the church today, if we let it. In 1838, Charles Dickens wrote *Nicholas Nickleby*, which tells the story of a young brother and sister who lose their father very early in life and a little later lose their mother. As the tale is told, eventually Nicholas takes care of his sister, the woman he desires to take as a wife, and the disabled orphan he befriends. At the end of the movie adaptation, the narrator sums up the story: "What happens when too early we lose a parent, that party on whom we rely for only everything? We must build a new family, person by person." That's what Jesus asks us to do, build a new family, person by person.

Who will raise our children?

Who will care for our elderly?

When we discuss "family values," whose family values are we discussing?

# Summary: Family on the Model

As can be expected, family looks very different on both sides of the model. According to the Individualistic extreme, family is defined as husband, wife, and children. There may be some abnormalities, such as divorce, but the norm is husband, wife, and children. In this structure, the individual is paramount. When the time comes to plan the family, ideally the husband and wife will decide when and how many children to have. The parents raise their children to become independent and leave home, building eventually an independent family of their own. Parents will take care of themselves as long as they are able, with money from retirement and IRAs. When they are no longer able to care for themselves, they will move into a retirement or nursing facility.

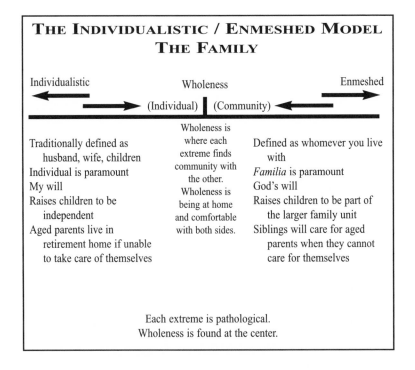

THE INDIVIDUALISTIC / ENMESHED MODEL
THE FAMILY

| Individualistic | Wholeness | Enmeshed |
|---|---|---|
| (Individual) | | (Community) |
| Traditionally defined as husband, wife, children | Wholeness is where each extreme finds community with the other. | Defined as whomever you live with |
| Individual is paramount | | *Familia* is paramount |
| My will | | God's will |
| Raises children to be independent | Wholeness is being at home and comfortable with both sides. | Raises children to be part of the larger family unit |
| Aged parents live in retirement home if unable to take care of themselves | | Siblings will care for aged parents when they cannot care for themselves |

Each extreme is pathological.
Wholeness is found at the center.

According to the Enmeshed extreme, family is defined as whomever you live with. This includes grandparents, aunts, uncles, and possibly the woman who has just emigrated from Mexico. In this structure, relationships are paramount, and networking is used to find jobs and housing. "Family planning" is left up to God, who decides when and how many children the family will be blessed with. The parents (and grandparents and aunts and uncles) raise the children in the knowledge that they will enlarge their family. It is assumed that the children, the oldest first, will take care of their elderly parents.

# Notes

[1] David Goetz, "Suburban Spirituality," *Christianity Today*, June 23, 2003.

[2] Beth Rushing, and Annette Schwabe, "The Health Effects of Work and Family Characteristics: Gender and Race Comparisons," *Sex Roles*, Vol. 33, 1995, 59-205.

[3] Michelle Conlin, "Unmarried America," *Business Week*, Oct. 20, 2003, 109.

[4] Clarence Page, "If Only Weddings Equaled Commitment," *The Arizona Republic,* Nov. 14, 2002.

[5] Alexandra Starr, "Washington's $1 Billion Lecture to the Poor," *Business Week*, Oct. 20, 2003, 116.

[6] Mike Littwin, "A 'Family-Values' Governor's Marriage Falls Apart," *Rocky Mountain News*, Sep. 2, 2003.

[7] Ibid.

[8] My point here is not to single out The Men's Wearhouse as being worse than everyone else. They're not.

[9] Mort Zuckerman, "All Work and No Play," *US News & World Report,* Sep. 8, 2003.

[10] Bob Herbert, "Caught in the Credit Card Vise," *The New York Times,* Sep. 22, 2003.

# Chapter 4

## *Education: The Pill for Every Ill*

"If you can read this, thank a teacher." Everyone is familiar with, if not the bumper sticker, at least the sentiment. Teachers are one of the most overlooked, overworked, underpaid vocational groups in the nation, and everyone recognizes the debt they owe to teachers. Did I say everyone? Well, not quite.

Teachers are dealt their fair share of blame for the problems plaguing our country. Teachers, some would say, especially in higher education, are liberal, touchy-feely people who are pushing their agenda on our children. What America needs is a return to good old-fashioned education – translate that into "the kind I got when I was a kid."

There is hardly anything of which America is prouder than its educational system. Whatever problems we might experience in our country, we've always had a firm belief that more education would solve it. Like Jan Amos Comenius, the early father of modern education, we believe that education is the means to achieve human potential. President Lyndon Johnson said, "The answer for all our national problems comes down to one single word, education." Poverty? Solution: better education for minorities. Teen-age pregnancy? Solution: better sex education at a younger age. AIDS? Solution: better sex education, period.

If education is the traditional, and to some the most obvious, solution to a plethora of problems, the pill for every ill, then it had better remain healthy itself. So what happens, then, when this system that we've placed all our trust in fails? What happens when the wheels come off and the system appears to have broken down?

For example, if school is traditionally the problem-solver, why do some studies show that affluent suburban teenagers, who typically have better schools, have more serious drug problems than inner-city teenagers? According to a study done by Teacher's College at Columbia University and Yale University,

> Suburban youths reported significantly higher levels of alcohol and drug use than their inner-city counterparts. Among suburban girls, 46% admitted using an illicit drug at least once in the past year, compared with 26% of inner-city females. And 59% of suburban boys used an illicit drug at least once, vs. 33% of boys in the inner city. Substance use was linked to personal distress among suburban youths but not inner-city youths. Researchers suggest that more suburban teens use drugs and alcohol to alleviate anxiety that may be caused partly by the high expectations of family and school officials. . . . suburban youths may have more pressure to succeed academically and particpate in co-curricular activities. Inner-city parents are just as likely to push for academic excellence, but other concerns,

such as poverty or unemployment, compete for attention.[1]

As we've seen with other issues, the changing demographics shift the way this particular issue fits on the model. The education system is undergoing some massive changes, and yet colleges still prepare teachers the way they've always prepared them. During the last twenty years, they've added more "touchy-feely" training to their curriculum before they get into the classroom. The real battle now is to remove that stuff and bring them back to basics.

As we'll see on the model, the Individualistic extreme leans heavily on the "back to basics" rhetoric, while the Enmeshed extreme propagates self-esteem. In the area of education, though, the highly individualistic, conservative extreme has really missed the understanding of where education is heading. Their desire is to move back to where education was in the 1950s and '60s – in other words, you need to learn how to speak English, how to read, and how to give change back from a dollar. Realistically, you don't need those skills today. You can work for Burger King and Wal-Mart and push the little button with a picture of a hamburger on it, and it rings it up and gives change. It's all done for you. Some, of course, will say, "But you can't say that people giving change at Burger King are successful." Once again, it depends on your definitions. To those poor who have crossed the borders into this country, the money made by working at Burger King looks like great wealth. Before looking at where education is heading, let's look at where it has been.

# A Brief History of Public Education

## Why It Was Started

Since their inception, schools have always been asked to do more than just teach certain subjects to children. In the excellent PBS series *The Merrow Report*, John Merrow states, "Education means more than academics. Americans have always asked public schools to do more than teach the basics. We've asked the public schools to assimilate immigrants, fight communism, end racism, wage war against poverty, and win the space race."[2]

At the beginning of the United States, many of our forefathers believed that the only way to secure a democracy was through the education of its citizenry. Benjamin Rush, a member of Congress and signer of the Declaration of Independence, believed that all citizens should have a supreme regard for the United States and believed that public education would teach and reinforce this regard. He said, "Our schools of learning, by producing a general, and more uniform system of education, will render the mass of the people more homogeneous."[3]

In order to create a homogeneous people (in other words, people that look like "us"), schools were needed that would be available to everyone, rich and poor alike. The first state-funded school of this sort (called normal or common, what we would today call public) was started in Massachusetts in 1839. Another purpose of the common school was religious indoctrination. Believing that a democracy was possible only with a moral populace, the founders established schools to teach the Scriptures along with other subjects.

To exaggerate a bit for just a moment, public education has been used for years as a propaganda machine, and what we propagated for many years was the American Dream.

Our schools taught family values. We learned about America and charity and generosity. We learned to say The Pledge of Allegiance and to sing "America the Beautiful." We learned respect. We learned the language, the culture, and the economic drive of what it meant to be American. The school system at its heart was used to say very clearly to its students, "Respect those things that are American," as though other countries couldn't claim such ideals. What the public school system put forth was the Individualistic extreme.

If public education was used as a propaganda machine, and the propaganda at the time was Individualistic, what happened when the country started changing? Right. The propaganda changed.

## What It Became

As the culture started to change, and we started to become more global and saw more cultural change and more immigration, the teachers, who were the best educated people in the country, changed and got ahead of the curve. They started teaching things that were more toward the center or even to the left of center. In other words, they started to teach things that are important to the growing number of people on the Enmeshed side of the model. They began to teach family planning, sex education, and self-esteem. Attitudes, feelings, and self-directed goals became the watchwords. Teachers emphasized cooperative learning, working together on projects, and put less stress on grades. Those on the other extreme are now complaining that it has become too "touchy-feely." We've moved away from what we felt should be taught, success, and now we're teaching community instead. The Individualistic extreme views public education as no longer working, as a broken institution. Never mind that our kids are learning how to use computers in the first grade. My seven-year-old granddaughter is more computer literate than I am. We're teaching them phenomenal things.

The battle is on, and the teacher's union has become the enemy. The teacher's associations and unions have become the strongest unions in the country, because they've moved to the Enmeshed extreme, and that's where the largest part of the population is. They are also the group that has been demonized most by the Individualistic extreme, because they've supposedly ruined public education, because they're "touchy-feely," because they're liberal. As noted by The (National Education Association) NEA and the AFT:

> Politically, teacher unions are major players at all levels of government. One of every ten delegates to the 1992 Democratic National Convention was a member of the NEA or the AFT, and no serious observer doubts their important role in state and local politics. Inasmuch as elected officials shape policy on noneducational as well as educational issues, the political influence of teacher unions extends far beyond the field of education. Although teacher unions are usually the most influential interest group on educational issues, their impact on noneducational issues may be even more important from a public policy perspective.

Most of the people arguing on this extreme about family and education are of an older generation. Conservatives such as Bill O'Reilly, Jerry Falwell, Rush Limbaugh, and Pat Robertson are members of that vocal group who espouse going back to "when it worked." Presumably, education has quit working because schools are teaching this kind of curriculum. So public education is the enemy. The problem is that the propaganda changed, and we want to go back to the old propaganda. So we're going to build charter schools or work toward a vouchers program or home school, so we can teach to people on the Individualistic extreme and raise our children to be "successful." Once again, we have people on both sides of the model pulling toward the extremes rather than pulling toward the center. The result? Nothing gets done.

# The Individualistic Reaction

## The Revisionist Charge

One of the charges leveled against the current state of education is that it is revisionistic. Conservatives accuse liberals of wanting to remove George Washington from the history books. What about the reports of Thomas Jefferson owning slaves or having a mistress who was a slave? That's revising history.

If you recall the discussion in chapter two about colonization, the first step of the colonizer is to rewrite history. Disengage people from their communities, make them forget their traditions, their stories, the ties that make them unique. By revising or rewriting their history, the colonizer begins to redefine the colonized from the outside. So the conservatives are angry because they view educators as revisionists. Not only do educators want to remove George Washington and add negative portrayals of Thomas Jefferson, but they also want to add stories about African-American leaders. Outrageous! That's rewriting history.

What's happening in education is that African Americans are finding African-American heroes and are writing about them. For instance, many children study astronauts in school, and for a great many children, an astronaut is what they want to be when they grow up. It is a childhood dream, serving America while also serving humanity, leading a life of integrity, bravery, and heroism. But while many of us grow up learning the names and deeds of Alan Shephard, John Glenn, Scott Carpenter, and Gus Grissom, how many of us have studied – or even know – that the first African-American astronaut was Robert Lawrence, Jr., or that the first African American to go into space was Guion Bluford, Jr.? If we study African-American history at all, it is most likely from the Civil War era (Frederick Douglass or Harriet Tubman) with maybe a few Civil Rights era people thrown in (Rosa Parks or Martin Luther King, Jr.). Do we study the African Americans who are making an impact on the world today?

Victor Davis Hansen, the author of *Mexifornia*, and I went through educational systems that subscribed to the same values, but we came out with very different views of what assimilation is about. He came out with a view that Latinos, in his case Mexicans, can assimilate and be made Americans. I came out realizing that no matter how much I assimilated, I would never be white. I began questioning, aren't there any Latinos who did anything noteworthy, who contributed to the sum of human knowledge, who did heroic things? Of course there are, but as soon as Latinos begin talking and writing about them, they were charged with the revisionist argument.

The point is, we've been revisionist from the beginning. Take the story of George Washington not lying about cutting down the cherry tree. Depending on your age, you learned about that in elementary school. But it's a myth, a story told to illustrate truthfulness and integrity. When we try to write history books without that, and with the stories of African Americans and Latinos and Asian Americans, the Individualistic side says, "You're trying to remove George

Washington from the history books." No, we just want to give him a page and a half like we give everybody else. Educator E.D. Hirsch writes:

> Those who have power in the present determine what shall be selected and interpreted from the infinite past. There is simply too much past to give students an endless history that is irrelevant to current realities. Events of recent years have redistributed power in the United States, and it is this change that lies behind the new multicultural redefinition of American history and literature. So long as Blacks and Asians and Latinos remained invisible in our present they also remained invisible in our past. But the present has changed, and henceforth so must the past.[4]

My greatest fear is not that we're rewriting history. It is that the educational system is breaking down further and further. Because of the revisionist argument, those on the Individualistic extreme are reacting by pulling their children out of the public school system and placing them in private and charter schools, or in the case of many Christians, homeschooling their children.

Several years ago, I was in Los Angeles speaking at a conference about educational issues. I said I was opposed to vouchers because I see schools segregating in an unhealthy way. Schools will start up to teach Latino history and others will teach African-American history. There will be less and less teaching of American history with a full complement of all its contributors. It will become so segmented, so fragmented, that people will start their own little ghettoized schools.

After the discussion, two African Americans came up to me and said that that was one of the reasons they were supporting the vouchers program and the charter school movement. It would give them an opportunity to teach the African-American way of thinking. It would also give them the opportunity to teach Muslim beliefs. When we talk about vouchers, most of the time we're thinking along the Individualistic extreme line; conservative Christians have been some of the biggest backers of this movement. So what happens when the schools that are being started are Muslim schools? I'm betting it will become a bit more controversial then and not so appealing!

Public education was established as part of the melting pot ideal, as part of assimilation, to get us together. It has done a creditable job over the years. Now, however, because more people are on the Enmeshed extreme, that's where education is moving. In an effort to bring it back the other way, the Individualistic extreme is basically dismantling public education. We're going back to the idea of teach your own kids what you want to teach them. Some people who are arguing against the current educational system are saying that bilingual education will make us another Canada. I'm suggesting that the vouchers and charter schools will make us another Canada. That is what is dividing us, and that is the key issue.

## Vouchers: What's Your School of Choice?

The voucher program, sometimes known as the free educational market model, provides tax-funded money to families in order for them to choose to which school to send their children. According to some, the problems in education are caused by the system being run by the government. That is what has allowed standards to become sloppy and for liberals to take over in the classroom. What is needed is for education to become a competitive market. Arguments state that as it purportedly does with the economy, competition will force standards up and will weed out poorly performing schools and teachers. For many, then, vouchers would be a way to get government funding for private, often times religious, schools.

The National Education Association (NEA) opposes the use of vouchers. For one, they argue, tax money that could be put toward improving schools would be diverted to private schools. Second, they assert that it is unconstitutional for the government to give money to religious organizations.

When you look at the vouchers movement, it has always been driven by the Individualistic extreme. For a good portion of white America – and the Individualistic extreme is still predominantly white – the solution is to move away from the Enmeshed extreme. White Americans tried to get away first by moving from the inner city to the suburbs. That didn't work because the minorities followed them; they wanted their own piece of the pie, and the Individualistic extreme was saying that the real pie was out in the suburbs. (Now that large numbers of minorities have moved out of the inner city, whites are moving back in and turning part of the inner city into high-priced lofts, apartments, and homes.) The vouchers program is the latest in the Individualistic approach to stay in power and stay away from the powerless – we'll develop our own schools or we'll homeschool.

Until 2003, no matter when the voucher issue came up on political ballots, it never passed. Liberals have always fought against vouchers, believing that it would create too much elitism and segregation. So the strategy changed, and voucher supporters pushed the idea that vouchers were for the poor, the struggling, the minorities in the inner cities. That put liberals in a difficult position, because it made it seem as though they were arguing against better education for the poor. It is clear, though, that vouchers would give money to taxpayers to help offset private school tuition. The fact that it wouldn't pay for tuition in full puts private schools once again out of the reach of the poor. So, tax money will be given to schools that don't need it and taken away from schools that do.

Further, the NEA doesn't accept the argument that vouchers are meant to help the poor. In laying out a social case against vouchers, it said:

> A voucher lottery is a terrible way to determine access to an education. True equity means the ability for every child to attend a good school in the neighborhood... . Vouchers were not designed to help low-income children. Milton Friedman, the "grandfather" of vouchers, dismissed the notion that vouchers could help low-income families, saying "it is essential that no conditions be attached to the acceptance of vouchers that interfere with the freedom of private enterprises to experiment." . . . A pure voucher system would only encourage economic, racial, ethnic, and religious stratification in our society. America's success has been built on our ability to unify our diverse populations. . . . Despite desperate efforts to make the voucher debate about "school choice" and improving opportunities for low-income students, vouchers remain an elitist strategy. From Milton Friedman's first proposals, through the tuition tax credit proposals of Ronald Reagan, through the voucher proposals on

ballots in California, Colorado, and elsewhere, privatization strategies are about subsidizing tuition for students in private schools, not expanding opportunities for low-income children.

In April 2003, though, Colorado passed a voucher measure, becoming the first to utilize school vouchers since the United States Supreme Court ruled that it is constitutional. For a while it looked like 20,000 students would be allowed to take their state money to private schools by the 2007-08 school year. By October 2003, thirty schools in Jefferson County, and thirty to forty in Denver could have applied for such funds. And it wasn't just Christian schools. It could also have been for African-American schools and Latino schools and Asian-American schools. And Muslim schools. Former pop star Cat Stevens spoke to a group of American Muslims at a Chicago convention recently. He urged them to start Muslim schools in their communities. "Once a Muslim school is established it indicates the arrival of the community in that place," he said.v However, I want to see what happens when we have forty Muslim schools applying, because I'm willing to bet there will be some serious debate then – and not just from conservative Christians in these post-September 11 days.

As it happens, though, we'll have to wait a bit longer to hear the debates about non-Christian religious schools. On December 3, 2003, Denver District Judge Joseph Meyer ruled that the school voucher law is indeed unconstitutional, because it strips local school boards of control over education.

The problem comes down once again to the powerful and powerless structure, the Individualistic/Enmeshed model. How do we deal with the fact that the powerful and the powerless are in the same classroom? We've tried to separate them as much as possible. We take the best teachers and move them to the nice new schools with the most resources, and we dump what's left to teach the powerless. Then when we do that, we come back and say that the education system has failed. Look at the numbers, we say. Kids in the inner city, mainly African Americans and Latinos, have huge dropout rates. They're failing in large numbers. The schools score low on standardized tests. And with the current "No Child Left Behind" program set in place by President George W. Bush, those schools that need the government funding the most will lose out because their scores are too low.

Part of what is happening is that some in the minority community are supporting vouchers. What they're saying is, "Once we have vouchers approved and our people can take the vouchers wherever they want, we can come in then and set up Latino schools and African-American schools. We can hire our own teachers and do our own thing." Homeschooling offers the same thing but from a predominantly religious stance.

Public education will look significantly different in the coming years if vouchers become universal. It will be everyone doing their own thing, segregating further into the powerful and the powerless, into the "us vs. them." Instead of coming to the center, we're trying to fix a broken model by moving further to the extremes. Breaking the system further, however, isn't going to heal it.

# The Curriculum

## Outcome Based Education

Beginning in the 1960s and continuing until just five or six years ago, an innovative program decided the curriculum in the public school system. Known as "outcome based education" or OBE, this program focused on the student rather than on the content learned. It was put forth that students may have different learning styles, so teachers and content ought to reflect that through different teaching styles.

Because this program arose during a time of tremendous racial upheaval, one of the most important goals became for members of all races and nationalities to get along in society. Foreshadowing Rodney King's plaintive cry of "Can't we just all get along?" the curriculum in public schools began to teach self-esteem and respect or tolerance of differing viewpoints. These things are critical to the hyphenated (African-, Mexican-, Asian-, etc.) Americans' learning and to their development: self-esteem, working within a community, the "it takes a village" mentality. And these are exactly the things that the powers-that-be become anxious about, because these concepts can't be tested.

## Back to Basics

High on the agenda of the Individualistic extreme is the "back to basics" movement. The OBE's emphasis on self-esteem and goal-setting is difficult to test. It's impossible to evaluate self-esteem on a test, because there are no hard, objective facts. This, of course, is what has led the Individualistic extreme to label OBE as "touchy-feely," and to state that the country's education has gone to hell because it has moved to the more Enmeshed extreme. The problem then becomes, how do we move education back from the Enmeshed side to the Individualistic side, to the Individualistic model of teaching. Thus "back to basics" was born.

"Back to basics" emphasizes the need for and the supremacy of the "three rs" – reading, 'riting, and 'rithmetic. Those three subjects are easy to evaluate. We can determine whether or not a student is learning the content or not by testing. Parents can see how well or how poorly their children are doing based on the grades that are sent home. The use of this grading system gives us the percentile on such nationwide tests as the Iowa Test of Basic Skills and other standardized assessment tests. It's not enough for the Individualistic extreme to simply learn math; the question is where is the student percentile-wise in the country? It's the percentile that is going to determine what college Janie is going to be eligible for, or whether Johnny should enhance his football skills.

Some schools have tried to do away with the grading system. Instead of A, B, C, D, or F, teachers will give out plus, check, or minus marks. It doesn't take a genius to figure out how the marks correspond to grades. So while these schools may be trying to move in a different direction, they are still working on the same model of testing and grades.

You can always tell who the highly Individualistic students are in school when you take a pass/fail course, especially at the university level. They're the ones bothering the professor with questions such as, "But how did I really do?" How can you be competitive, how can you know that you did better than everyone else if you don't have a letter grade or percentage to prove it?

When I was in seminary, I had a counseling professor with whom I developed a close relationship. He would come into class, open his file folder, and teach the entire class time flipping through pages and writing notes on the board. One time, I went up to talk to him after class, and I looked at his file folder. It had nothing to do with the class he was teaching. He said, "If I come in here and just wing it, people get uptight, like I'm not prepared." He said once that I was the only student who never challenged him on a grade or asked for a grade change. Some students will argue about the one- or two-point difference between a B+ and an A-. He asked me about it. I told him that I always assumed that grades were for the teachers. It's what makes them feel that they're doing their job, or it helps them to evaluate whether they've communicated a concept clearly enough. (In other words, if everybody gets an F, the professor had better look at some ways to make it clearer!) I've never looked at grades as being that important. If I get an A or a C, I'm not going to learn anything else by arguing over my grade. I've already learned what I'm going to learn. If I get a B+ instead of an A-, I'm not going to learn anything else by convincing the professor to give me one extra point. It's not the grades that matter; it's the learning.

One of the biggest differences between the Individualistic extreme and the Enmeshed extreme is the emphasis on grades. Those on the Individualistic extreme work for the grades and eventually for the piece of paper that tells them they're good enough. They don't necessarily work for the learning. And yet, what else is schooling for? Albert Einstein understood the difference between learning and just getting the grade. He said, "One should guard against preaching to young people success in the customary form as the main aim in life. The most important motive for work in school and in life is pleasure in work, pleasure in its result, and the knowledge of the value of the result to the community." He knew that in order for a society to survive, the individual and the community must come together, that to sacrifice the community to Individualistic goals would mean the corruption and eventual destruction of society. Note how he blends the individual with the community: "Never regard study as a duty, but as the enviable opportunity to learn to know the liberating influence of beauty in the realm of the spirit *for your own personal joy* and *to the profit of the community* to which your later work belongs" (emphasis mine). This doesn't mean the individuals are destroyed, but that they work together cooperatively rather than competitively. "Desire for approval and recognition is a healthy motive; but the desire to be acknowledged as better, stronger, or more intelligent than a fellow human being or fellow scholar easily leads to an excessively egoistic psychological adjustment, which may become injurious for the individual and for the community."[6]

The "back to basics" movement has moved from public schools into the colleges and universities as well. David Horowitz recently spoke in Denver about his "academic bill of rights." His argument is that because professors in universities have all become liberal, "touchy-feely" people, we need to have more conservatives in education. So we need to get more people who are teaching "back to basics" subjects. Horowitz argues that his bill of rights isn't about filling a quota but simply asking that professors offer all points of view on such things as political arguments. And yet, listening to Horowitz talk, one doesn't hear much of any other point of view from him either. Apparently, what's good for the liberal goose is not good for the conservative gander.

One thing that Horowitz and other conservatives like him don't seem to realize is that most conservatives, or Individualistic people, don't want to be in academia because, with the exception of a few ivy-league institutions, that's not where the money is! For every Horowitz wanting conservatives to be in academia, we can find some who argue that they want more liberals to be CEOs of major corporations.

## No Child Left Behind

Going hand in hand with the "back to basics" movement

is the "No Child Left Behind" (NCLB) act, signed by Pres. George W. Bush in January 2002. This act intends to develop accountability for the academic achievement of students. States will set standards for what students at each grade level should know in reading, math, and science.

One goal of NCLB is that disadvantaged families living in poor neighborhoods with poor schools will be able to send their children to a school of their choice. It doesn't address, however, how that child is supposed to get to the other school and back home again. Jamie McKenzie, editor of the anti-NCLB e-zine "No Child Left," notes,

> Despite decades of evidence that poor school performance is shaped in part by poverty, neglect and various social disadvantages, NCLB does little to alter those root causes. Anyone with a true commitment to turning around the performance of disadvantaged children would address all aspects of the malfunctioning system, from housing, employment and medical care to pre-schooling (Head Start) and school improvement.[7]

Several other problems exist with NCLB. First, it emphasizes testing in reading and math. If a school performs well in these areas, federal funding is received. Theoretically, a school could do well in these limited areas and poorly in others. By rewarding these subjects, we are guaranteeing poorer performance in other subjects. What's happened, then, to a well-rounded education? As McKenzie states,

> NCLB's focus on just math and reading scores could have a profoundly

undemocratic effect upon a generation of students in poorly performing schools, as schools may strip away much of the broad education that is their birthright in order to elevate scores on just two indicators. Students in affluent schools with good scores may continue to enjoy a full range of subjects including art, social studies and science, while disadvantaged students are condemned to a second class education putting "Reading First" at the expense of a complete education. This preoccupation with LITERACY over all else sets up an increasingly two class society, with one group condemned to a lean diet of basic skills and the other getting the more complete diet associated with power and success in this society.

Once again, the powerful become more powerful while the powerless suffer.

Second, if families are allowed to transfer students to better performing schools, what will be done about overcrowding? Nothing.

Third, what will NCLB do to disabled students? Currently, the Individuals with Disabilities Education Act (IDEA) guarantees disabled people an education. While money promised to support the program (40 percent of the cost) has not been met, it's better than nothing, and IDEA believes that No Child Left Behind will indeed leave some children behind: those with disabilities.

Finally, there is no way to test some of the subjects that OBE has deemed important, such as self-esteem. You can't test "touchy-feely" subjects with a standard, fill-in-the-bubble, multiple-choice test. Currently, the NCLB Act is stating that the government is going to test everybody and if the schools don't make the cut, the government won't give them federal funds. The fact of the matter is, a lot of schools aren't going to make it. If they lose federal funds, the state is going to move faster toward vouchers for charter schools and private schools. The government doesn't care where you get your education as long as you get one. So, as I noted earlier, we'll wind up with each group teaching its own thing, and no one receiving a well-rounded, complementary education.

# Alternative Education

## The Dropout Rate

Playing into all the arguments about education is the high dropout rate of Hispanics and African Americans. While I don't want to downplay the seriousness of these statistics, I do, however, want to offer some alternative explanations. First, the statistics.

According to The Merrow Report, about 30 percent of all Latinos, immigrants and native-born, drop out or never enroll in school. The number will only increase, it says, because Latinos under the age of eighteen are the fastest growing demographic group. In contrast, 9 percent of whites and 12 percent of blacks drop out of high school. While some of the problem may be due to difficulties with language and a still-racist system, this study proposes that a possible reason for the high dropout rate may be the lack of a compelling future. Carlos Jimenez, a teacher in the California school system, when asked about the lack of imagination of what to become in the future, said:

> Part of it probably does have to do with a
> curriculum that is . . . always studying about

somebody else. . . . I think it's a disgrace that kids in the United States are more familiar with Egyptian pyramids than they are of Mexican pyramids. . . . We're completely ignorant of that country, its history, the people. And I think it has devastating effects on the young people in terms of their own self-image.[8]

A student comments, "You don't know your history. You don't know where you come from. You don't know what to be proud of."

In the statistics about drop-out rate, education is described as from nursery school, kindergarten through college or anything preparing someone for college level or above education. It doesn't include trade or vocational schools. This is a clear indication of the Individualistic extreme where success isn't defined by someone going to a trade school. That skews the statistics somewhat.

Currently, Latinos have a high dropout rate, because the system is already breaking down. You don't need a college degree to run a construction company. If you travel up to Vail, Colorado, you will see the number of people building extremely fancy homes; the majority of the workers bulding those homes are Mexicans, not even United States-born Latinos but Mexicans. They may not know how to speak English, and they certainly don't have a high-school diploma, but they know how to lay marble tile. Their kids are probably going to drop out of school when they're sixteen, because they can go work with Dad laying marble tile and make a lot more money than they can make with a high-school education. We don't have a way of tracking them, other than to say they're dropouts.

If we have a 50 percent dropout rate for Hispanics, we have to deal with the question of how it is that this group can have that dropout rate and still have the fastest growing per capita income of any group in the country. There has been a 36.4 percent increase in per capita income for Hispanics in the past decade, a 118 percent rise in purchasing power, and a median income of $33,447 in 2000.[9] According to *Hispanic Business*, of Hispanic households with two or more earners, 43.2 percent make between $40,000 and $79,999. It is the only income category in which Hispanics out-earn white non-Hispanics.[10]

The fact of the matter is, you don't need a high-school diploma, you don't need to go to college, to get by. You can live in America and live comfortably without a college education. If you can live without a college education, then the last two years of high school are lost years. We're still pushing college education for everyone. But too many can't afford it. Tuition keeps going up, and it's getting harder and harder to finance. What we need to realize is that not everyone wants or needs a college education.

## Trade or Vocational Schools

It becomes important, then, to be able to offer courses that may appeal to those who are looking at alternative vocations. For example, Parks Business School in Denver is the largest Hispanic "ghetto" in the city. Hispanics are pursuing degrees there in medicine, business, and criminal justice. Some are becoming probation officers, others paralegals.

My son David provides a good example of what is happening in some of these areas. David has a gift with students that I've never seen before. He's laid back with them, and yet he carries an authority in his air that makes them pay attention. David, though, was a poor student, and it was only by hook or crook that he finally graduated high school. Traditional college was out of the question. He eventually got a job as a paraprofessional in a local elementary school. And the students love him. He became good at being the "discipline guy." The teachers knew they could send a problem student to David, and he would work with that student one-on-one until the student was ready to go back into a group setting. David now is the coordinator of the Positive Alternatives for School Success program – a partnered program between HIS Ministries and Palmer Elementary School. He is going to Parks Business School and is getting his degree in criminal justice. Eventually, he'd like to take the PASS program that he designed and replicate it in other schools. He found a non-traditional approach that worked for him, and now he's helping students who might otherwise fall through the cracks.

Not everyone is going to go to college, and not everybody should go to college. If everyone went to college, we wouldn't have construction workers and street maintenance. So for those who are interested in heavy equipment, how do we teach them heavy equipment and have them come out of high school with a certificate to work for a heavy equipment company? Can you imagine the furor that would cause if we said that's what public education is going to look like? Shop has always been for losers, for those who can't do the "real" education stuff. Maybe it's time that changed.

An example of the training I'm talking about is the seminary education I received – or didn't receive. It was a great education as far as it went, but the nature of society is changing and education must change with it. Seminaries are still saying that everyone should learn Greek and Hebrew. But how many people remember those languages when they've been out of school for three or four years? Most pastors have software that can do all that for them. So instead of teaching seminary students Greek and Hebrew, why not train people to use the software? Most seminaries don't teach the practical things that pastors need to know. Haddon Robinson, the president of Denver Seminary when I was there and currently the Harold J. Ockenga Distinguished Professor of Preaching at Gordon-Conwell Theological Seminary, said that seminaries have never been good at training pastors. Years ago, seminaries sent out pastors with a lot of head knowledge but mediocre training, because the people in the church would whip that pastor into shape, and within six months the pastor would know everything he or she needed to know to run the church. The problem is that now, the people in the church aren't used to being in church either. Many of them are brand new, as well. So now the seminary sends out the mediocre pastors, and no one knows what to do with them!

Haddon tried to make changes in those areas and make seminary training more practical, but he came up against controversy every step of the way. The Individualistic extreme will not allow those changes to be made, because it is not head knowledge; it's too "touchy-feely." And it is this argument that is killing public schools.

## Theme Schools

An interesting development is in the area of theme schools. While maintaining a traditional curriculum, these schools offer courses in a particular theme to help attract students. Some of the themes are vocational, others are academic.

As the culture moves from Individualistic to Enmeshed, we'll have fewer corporations and more and more mom-and-pop shops. Possibly, there will be less need for science and business and more for the social arts. These are the kinds of subjects that the government is already working on eliminating from the education budget. Eventually, though, we might see theme schools that offer a traditional curriculum – the "back to basics" subjects – in addition to a heavy music curriculum including Spanish guitar or art or family relationships.

The North Kansas City School system has three theme schools, one for the automotive industry, one for carpentry, and one for information technology. Their promotional material states, "The goal of the academy is to ready students for immediate employment in the IT industry as well as to prepare them for post-secondary education." That's a visionary program – one that admits that not all students will want post-secondary education.

Some of the theme schools are working on being dual language programs. Bilingual programs have been argued over for years. They were started as a way to take immigrants from the Enmeshed extreme and bring them to the Individualistic extreme. It was intended for the immigrants to learn English and forget Spanish, for them to attain English fluency after three or four years. That didn't happen, of course. What happened was people became bilingual, fluent in both, so now there's a push to stop it. However, there is a school in Denver, Northstar Elementary, that teaches in both languages. It's not intended as a bridge for students to learn English and drop Spanish. It is a true bilingual program that intends for students to study bilingually. Many parents of academic-bound students want their children to be fluent in another language before hitting college. I know a missionary from Honduras who has just moved back to Denver. The parents are both white, and they have three children. They've looked all over the city for a school and have signed up at Northstar.

*Questions for Reflection*

Can we teach the mind and touch the heart?

How can we effect an extreme makeover of the mind and heart?

Who are the future teachers?

## Summary: Education on the Model

It is clear that education is in need of reform. Unfortunately, pulling to either the Individualistic or Enmeshed extremes doesn't make for good reform. What it makes for is a lot of arguing at the expense of true learning.

The Individualistic extreme places a high emphasis on degrees and, therefore, on testing and grades. Learning is of secondary importance. Because of this emphasis, students must learn things that can be tested, such as math, science, and reading. This has led to the "back to basics" movement and to governmental participation through the "No Child Left Behind" act. Traditional approaches to school include private and charter schools and homeschooling. While many Individualistic parents may send their child to public school, the emphasis is still on grades and school activities in preparation for college. Vouchers become an important part of this discussion as some see government money allowing them to send their children to a school that will emphasize "academic success."

The Enmeshed extreme places a high emphasis on learning rather than degrees. Students want to learn things that are important to them, whether that places them on a college-track or not. This means that more non-traditional approaches to schooling will arise, such as theme schools, vocational and trade schools. Because of the Enmeshed extreme's focus on community, it is important for the student to develop self-esteem and a place within community. Outcome-based education arose as a way to develop learning rather than testing. This has led to the charge of classes being too "touchy-feely," with things like self-esteem not being testable.

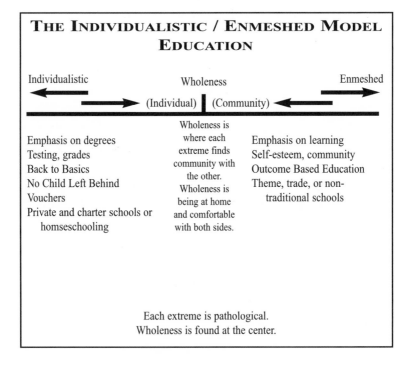

**THE INDIVIDUALISTIC / ENMESHED MODEL EDUCATION**

Individualistic — Wholeness — Enmeshed

(Individual) | (Community)

Emphasis on degrees
Testing, grades
Back to Basics
No Child Left Behind
Vouchers
Private and charter schools or homeschooling

Wholeness is where each extreme finds community with the other. Wholeness is being at home and comfortable with both sides.

Emphasis on learning
Self-esteem, community
Outcome Based Education
Theme, trade, or non-traditional schools

Each extreme is pathological.
Wholeness is found at the center.

112

# Notes

[1] Stephaan Harris, "Drug Use, Depression Break Through Suburban Walls: Mix of Pressure, Affluence Gets More Teens into Trouble," *USA Today*, Aug. 16, 1999, 05D.

[2] John Merrow, "In Schools We Trust," *The Merrow Report*.

[3] Benjamin Rush, "Thoughts Upon the Mode of Education Proper in a Republic."

[4] E.D. Hirsch, Jr., *Toward a Centrist Curriculum: Two Kinds of Multiculturalism in Elementary School* (Charlottesville, VA: Core Knowledge Foundation, 1992).

[5] "Cat Stevens Urges U.S. Muslims to Start Own Schools," *Denver Post*, Sep. 2, 2003.

[6] Albert Einstein, "On Education," an address at Albany, N.Y., on the occasion of the celebration of the tercentenary of higher education in America, October 15, 1936. Translated by Lina Arronet. Published in 'Out of My Later Years': New York, Philosophical Library, 1950. The full text of this address can be found online at info.chymes.org/Einstein/on_education.html.

[7] Jamie McKenzie, "Gambling with the Children," http://nochildleft.com/2003/jan03.html#index.

[8] John Merrow, "Lost in Translation," *The Merrow Report*.

[9] Laura Castaneda, "Getting a Piece of the Flan: Smart Marketing, Not Just Good Products, Is Needed to Earn a Piece of the $452 Billion Hispanic Market," *San Diego Metropolitan*, July 2002.

[10] "Hispantelligence Report," *Hispanic Business*, Nov. 2003, 16.

# Chapter 5

## Taking Care of Business?

We often hear that we shouldn't define ourselves by the work we do. Work is not our life. While that may seem to be good advice, it's hard to live by, particularly with the hours we put into our jobs. If you are a typical full-time employee, you put in 40 hours of work a week. That averages out to almost 25 percent of your time being spent at this thing that doesn't define you. If you are in management or are self-employed, that percentage is even higher.

Mort Zuckerman notes:

> We have become the developed world's leaders in nonstop work. It is not called the "American work ethic" for nothing. We not only work about 50 weeks a year; the average American works nearly 2,000 hours a year. Remember those hard-working Germans? They put in about 1,500 hours a year – a difference of almost three months of 40-hour workweeks. About 40 percent of Americans put in 50-hour workweeks. We even work about three weeks more a year

than the Japanese. Why do we put up with more limited vacation time than any other wealthy nation? Because we define ourselves more by our work. "Workaholic" in America is often a compliment. . . . The first question most people in America will ask a stranger is, "What do you do?" In much of Europe, this is considered inappropriate. We are proud of being busy – it is a virtue; being idle is perceived as a vice.[1]

What exactly, then, is this thing that we define ourselves by, and how is the changing demographics impacting it?

## Putting Business on the Model

While it might seem natural to put corporations on the Individualistic extreme and entrepreneurships on the Enmeshed extreme, the truth is that both are driven by the same thing: capitalism. The simplest definition of capitalism is an economic system in which goods and services are produced, owned, and exchanged by individuals with minimal government regulation. Within this definition are two key concepts to understanding capitalism. First, a free market determines pricing, so there is a clear separation (well, yes, at times a muddied separation) between business and state. Second, and this is the driving thrust of both corporations and entrepreneurships, individuals and companies are allowed to compete for their own economic gain.

### Defining Success

The difference between the Individualistic and the Enmeshed extremes is the ethics that drive them. While both are driven by capitalism, the Individualistic extreme operates in a highly competitive manner while the Enmeshed extreme sees competition as being "cut-throat." For example, the small business vendor selling tacos on a street corner has learned to accommodate the other seventeen small taco vendors in the same community. There isn't the drive to underprice the other guy and drive everyone else out of business. The ethic here says, "We can all do business together. I'll take these seven blocks, you take those seven blocks." Work isn't used to define anyone on the Enmeshed side. Work is to provide for the family, which in turn defines a person. The Enmeshed side is going to work enough to feed his or her family and take care of the family's needs. There is no need to work any more than that.

The Individualistic extreme, on the other hand, is driven by market share and is highly competitive. This ethic states, "If work defines who a person is, then I had better be successful. I need more and more, and I need a bigger piece of the market." This person then, either corporate or entrepreneurial, is driven by mergers and acquisitions. A person may start a little mom-and-pop store, but if that person comes from the Individualistic extreme, pretty soon it's not enough to have just one. So how do you build this one business so that you can start it up somewhere else and eventually have seven in the city? Make a better product, lower the prices, give better service. If you do those things, you can drive the others out of business.

A lot of companies right now are looking at the book *Good to Great: Why Some Companies Make the Leap . . . and Others Don't* by Jim Collins. Collins and his team of researchers sorted through a list of 1,435 companies, looking for those that made substantial improvements in their performance over time. *Good to Great* took eleven companies and tracked them to find out what made them great. Now, every business in the country is culling its pages, looking for the magic key to success, trying to do the same things. "Great" in Collins' book as well as elsewhere in American society is defined as bigger, more profitable, higher stock value, more production. In other words, the Individualistic extreme. I preached a sermon on this subject not too long ago, because the church has fallen into the same trap.ii The church wants to be successful by American standards. What makes a church great? The number of people in attendance, the size of the budget, and the size of the building. Bob Buford wrote a book called *Halftime* in which he suggests that we spend the first half of our lives driven by success, working for money and the things it buys, only to find out when we've succeeded, that we still feel empty. So we reinvent ourselves in the second half and desire to live a life that is driven by a search for significance. I suggest that Buford is writing about the Individualistic extreme.

At the Enmeshed extreme, "good to great" looks different. This extreme is already driven by significance, by relationship. Success is defined by relationships, so at this extreme, success means having customers who are loyal, who love your product or business, and who will come back forever because they like what you're doing. Businesses or entrepreneurships at this extreme are comfortable being small. Many of these people have set up their companies, not to grow or to be a great place of employment, but because they can make a comfortable living here. They don't need more. They can have a little house for the kids and a car. Why work for more than what you need?

## Business Structure and Benefits

Another difference between the two extremes is in the planning and structure of a business. On the Individualistic side, planning, capital structures, and financing all play into starting up a business. It's very hierarchical, even in small businesses. They're established with a three- or four-year plan and have people in charge of marketing, even in a small mom-and-pop restaurant. In order to grow bigger, a business always has to be planning five years down the road. In contrast, very few on the Enmeshed side deal with five-year plans. These are the people who are trying to deal with next week.

It used to be that when someone was offered a job, he or she took a good look at the benefits package. What kind of retirement package is being offered? What's the health insurance like? The dilemma for the Enmeshed extreme is they don't do that kind of planning. Let's say you're a twenty-five or thirty-year-old man who sets up a lawn-mowing company. You're successful enough that you hire people. You're always working on the theory that as you get older, you'll keep hiring younger and younger people to do the work that you can no longer do. There's no retirement. You'll keep the lawn-mowing company until you're ninety, but as long as you can keep hiring younger people, you can still operate it. What isn't planned for is the likelihood of injury or accident, which would mean not being able to run the company. That's a major dilemma.

To the Enmeshed extreme, retirement and health care look like fringe benefits, costly ones at that. When corners need to be cut in order to make ends meet, it is usually these fringes that get cut. A friend's brother, Mike, knows about this firsthand. In his twenties and just out of the Navy, Mike got a job as an electrician with a major contractor in Denver. Soon after learning the ropes – or the wires, in this case – Mike got his license and decided to go out on his own. He and a friend left the contractor and began doing business with Mike's wife doing the billing and accounting. Now it's thirty years later. Mike and his partner are doing well. Their employees are sons and sons-in-law. But Mike was recently diagnosed with multiple sclerosis. While he is still able to work, there is no guarantee that he won't be wheelchair bound or blind in five years, facing no retirement and no health care.

Currently, we may be facing an equalization in this country where those in the middle class are sinking into the same situations faced by those in the working class. Certain benefits such as health care are being cut in corporations as well. Corporations are finding that by hiring more temporary workers or part-time employees, they don't have to pay skyrocketing insurance costs. In the most recent (as of this writing) economic downturn, the person with a Ph.D. or an M.B.A. degree stood in the unemployment line with the "uneducated." Because companies don't want to pay out benefits, these people who were guaranteed a job by the American Dream now have to buy their own insurance and retirement plans. In some cases, they might not be making a lot more at the bottom line than our hypothetical man owning the lawn-mowing company. This adds even more stress to the dynamic of illegal immigration. The immigrants are making a bunch of money, and from the perspective of the native-born, the immigrants are taking their jobs.

Business has a lot to learn, and if it doesn't change as the times change, the economy will collapse. When you have a system that no longer works but you're trying to maintain the status quo with that same system, it falls apart. That's what happened to communism. It fell, and we say that the development is proof that communism doesn't work. But it didn't fail for that reason. I think what happened is that the Soviet Union was led by a group of people who were unwilling to change the institution. But the people changed. When they changed, the institution no longer worked, and communism fell. Let me give you an example that's closer to home.

# Savings and Loan:
# The Felling of an American Institution

It's helpful when thinking about the Savings and Loan (S&L) crisis, to think first about why they were started and how they differed from banks. The movie *It's a Wonderful Life* gives us a fair approximation of the business. George Bailey owned the Bailey Building and Loan while Mr. Potter owned the bank. The S&Ls, or thrifts as they were then called, were local lenders who helped working class people save for the purchase of a home. Banks, on the other hand, offered a wide array of services and products to individuals and corporations, while thrifts handled only mortgages. Remember in the movie when Potter is arguing with George about the Bailey Building and Loan? He mentions that the reason one of the "garlic eaters" had to get a loan from George was because the banks wouldn't give him one; he was a bad risk. George, when trying to save his business, reminds the man that the Building and Loan helped him build a home. "Do you think that Potter would have helped you? Do you think that when you were struggling and thought you might lose your house, do you think that Potter would have helped you? No." This attitude is consistent with the S&Ls. Thrifts believed that they were helping people become better citizens by making it easier to buy a home, and that it strengthened character when people were taught to save money. Bankers were viewed with suspicion, as people who were doing something only for a profit. Thrifts believed they were part of social reform.

Then a couple of events happened that presented challenges to the S&L industry. Occasionally, thrifts, and even banks, got into "rate wars" when thrifts raised the rates paid on savings in order to lure depositors. In 1966, these rate wars became so severe that Congress set limits on

121

savings rates. According to David Mason of Young Harris College:

> The thirteen years following the enactment of rate controls presented thrifts with a number of unprecedented challenges, chief of which was finding ways to continue to expand in an economy characterized by slow growth, high interest rates and inflation. . . . Because regulators controlled the rates thrifts could pay on savings, when interest rates rose depositors often withdrew their funds and placed them in accounts that earned market rates, a process known as disintermediation. At the same time, rising rates and a slow growth economy made it harder for people to qualify for mortgages that in turn limited the ability to generate income. In response to these complex economic conditions, thrift managers came up with several innovations, such as alternative mortgage instruments and interest-bearing checking accounts, as a way to retain funds and generate lending business. Such actions allowed the industry to continue to record steady asset growth and profitability during the 1970s even though the actual number of thrifts was falling.

By the late 1970s and into the '80s, interest rates had soared as did inflation because of the doubling of oil prices. This threatened the failure of the S&Ls, so Congress deregulated the S&L industry to allow thrifts to compete more effectively with banks and other financial institutions and to expand their lending authority. Mason notes that this was the first time the government had acted to promote profit rather than homeownership. Another change that deregulation brought about was allowing more lenient accounting rules.

The deregulation of the S&L industry led to lender misconduct and fraud. For example, the way S&Ls started competing with banks was to lend a higher percentage of the mortgage and give the buyer slack on the appraisal. So, the banks would say we'll lend you 80 percent, and the S&L would say we'll lend you 85 percent. Banks responded with an appraisal of the property at $150,000, and the S&L came back with an appraisal of $185,000. S&Ls were lending money on a building that would then be reappraised and resold. At that time, you could buy a building for $150,000 and sell it two weeks later for $250,000; S&Ls would put a mortgage on it, because that's the only way they could stay in business. Some S&Ls had a "go for broke" attitude toward making these high-risk loans. If the loan worked, of course, the S&L would make big money, but if the loan went bad, they reasoned that insurance would cover the losses. And because deregulation also meant a reduction in regulatory oversight, fraudulent S&Ls were able to avoid scrutiny. When we realized what had happened and the economy started going sour and people started trying to sell these buildings, they couldn't sell them for $185,000, and the S&Ls were left holding a lot of bad paper.

Banks were also trying to stay afloat during this pre-crisis time. They were seeing more business going to S&Ls than they wanted. With deregulation, other institutions, such as car dealerships, could give loans so that people didn't have to go to the bank. Banks began the risky venture of lowering their standards on loan applications in order to attract business. Further, they found a lucrative market in lending to other countries. And the attitude behind all the high-risk loans was that if the loan went sour, it would be backed by the FDIC.

The S&L crisis shows what happens when leaders try to give short-term answers, such as deregulation, to a longer-term problem. The institutions were changing, and the leaders didn't want to deal with the change. When you have a system that no longer works but you're trying to maintain the status quo with that same system, it falls apart. We're still dealing with the financial problems that the S&L crisis created. When the S&Ls collapsed, it was the taxpayers – you and me – who ended up footing the bill at a cost of nearly $500 billion.

The same thing happened with Enron. It was a major mistake for businesses to be paying executives based on the value of stock instead of on profit and money in the bank. The obvious way it was going to be done was for executives to find a way to pump up the value of stock whether they made money or not. So we had an economy that was running on stock values that were coming out of nowhere. Never before in the history of business had we given bonuses to people based on the value of stock. We had always given bonuses based on profits. If you earn the profit, then we'll give you a bonus. We changed it to giving stock options – if the value goes up by three points, you'll get another million shares. So the focus shifted from making a profit to finding ways to bump up the price of the stock. The Individualistic extreme took over. Enron executives found a way to bump the price of the stock, get their stock options, sell their options, and then when we got around to finding out that the stock wasn't worth that, it crashed. We found out that all these companies were in fact broke, but they were making billionaires at the top.

When things fall apart in a country, I'm not convinced that they fall apart because the systems were necessarily bad, but because the leadership didn't change the systems with the times. Communism fell apart because the system didn't change; it didn't have anything to do with goodness and badness. We didn't have anything to do with it. Communism didn't implode simply because it was a bad system. Rather, the leadership failed to change with the times. So, too, with the Individualistic extreme and businesses. Systems are changing, and if we refuse to change with them, we will implode.

## Taking Business Overseas

Many corporations are trying to deal with the changes in business by becoming global companies. The thinking seems to be that by taking advantage of the people not only of our own country but of other countries as well, then those companies can become huge and more successful than they've ever been. The multinational corporations have always taken advantage of poor people in other countries in order to become profitable. That will continue, and certain people will become richer and richer. The amazing thing is, we have poor in this country as well, but corporations can pay the poor in other countries less than they can here, and they get tax breaks for doing so.

The argument is that if a corporation takes its business overseas, then they don't have to pay minimum wage. People can't live today on minimum wage. At an average of $6 per hour, forty hours per week, an individual can make $240 per week. That may be a good wage for a teenager, but a family of four can't make it on that. If mom and dad both work, that raises the weekly income to $480, which is still at or below the poverty level. Corporations, however, have said that they can't continue to do business if the minimum wage is raised. They'll just take their business elsewhere. The minimum wage issue has been a huge battle in politics.

The Democrats say that raising minimum wage will help the poor and increase their standard of living, so let's set it higher. The other side says simply, "we'll take our business elsewhere." That's been the trade-off, and in the meantime, as with other issues, nothing is getting done.

But even more than the interminable arguments about minimum wage, work done overseas simply costs less. The savings for an American company can be as much as 50 percent. "That is the message of the nation's management consultants, who are encouraging their corporate clients to take advantage of the multiplying opportunities overseas . . . . 'What we are basically saying is that if your competitors are doing this, you will be at a disadvantage if you don't do it too.'"[3]

Did you catch the Individualistic strain running through that quote? Be competitive, be cut-throat; if you don't, you will be left behind and you will be unsuccessful. For the Enmeshed group, globalization isn't that big of a thing. They're not going to sell churros anywhere else other than their street corner. They may be impacted by the prices on the open market, as we all are, but they're not concerned with making the CEO richer. It's a simple operation. The more complex you are, the less competition you have. So the Individualistic corporations will drive away competition by pricing, by complex structures, by the ability to be a global company and to have global financing or to open a branch in China. At the Enmeshed extreme, none of that comes into play.

The off-shoring of U.S. jobs has also contributed to the rise in the unemployment rate.

> By these initial estimates, at least 15 percent of the 2.81 million jobs lost in America since the decline began have reappeared overseas. Productivity improvements at home —

sustaining output with fewer workers — account for the great bulk of the job loss. But the estimates being made suggest that the work sent overseas has been enough to raise the unemployment rate by four-tenths of a percentage point or more, to the present 6.1 percent.[4]

One group estimates that by 2015, 3.3 million jobs will have been eliminated.

What we're going to have to look at in order to keep from going broke is a tax policy that says to these corporations, moving positions offshore is fine, but for every job you take out of this country, we're going to charge an appropriate amount in taxes. That would stop it in a minute. But part of what we've done is we've allowed them to move the jobs somewhere else and continue to increase the salaries of CEOs, and exploit the poor in other countries.

Howard Dean, who sought the Democratic presidential nomination in early 2004, raised some interesting issues during his bid to be the democratic candidate. He talked about taxation for people who take jobs elsewhere. Further, he said that we should expect corporations to give the same benefits to workers in Taiwan as in Tucson. He also said, and received a lot of negative feedback about it, that it's time we allow unions to follow these companies into other countries.

This country is great because of the labor movement. The union movement built the middle class. . . . We should never have a free trade agreement without labor and environmental standards. The necessary condition of free trade is not just to develop industrial capacity in the Third World, but also to develop a middle class there. Therefore, if it's OK for GM to move to Mexico and open a plant, it is OK for the UAW to organize that plant.[5]

Let's face it. If we really wanted to stop the illegal immigration of Mexicans to the United States, we would unionize the companies that the United States has in Mexico. Mexicans wouldn't come here, then, because they'd have equal or better jobs there.

I'm convinced that in the next several years we'll see the companies that have taken their business overseas go under because of quantity of product. One of the reasons we've always had the benefit of how we do business is that we had all the knowledge here in the United States of how to do it. We never exported the knowledge, only the labor. However, if you're making Levis in Thailand, it's not going to take long for the workers in Thailand to figure out how Levis are made. And they can make them for a lot less if their whole operation is there than if the corporate offices are in New York. Further, because of the global village we live in, created in large part by the Internet, the people in Thailand can sell jeans from there just as easily as they can from anywhere else. Maybe someone can argue that the quality of the Levis made in Albuquerque would be better, but I'm not convinced that Americans turn out a better product simply by virtue of being American.

Most of the jobs that have gone overseas are middle-class jobs, a great many in manufacturing, which contributes to the declining middle class in this country. However, skilled jobs are beginning to transfer overseas as well, including such workers as aeronautical engineers and software developers. "Intel itself has maintained a fairly steady 60 percent of its employees in the United States. But in the past year or so, it has added 1,000 software engineers in China and India, doing work that in the past might have been done by people hired in the United States. 'To be competitive, we have to move up the skill chain overseas,' Mr. [Craig R., chief executive of Intel] Barrett said."[6]

Two significant movements are combining to eliminate the middle class, which in turn creates a greater gap between the powerful and the powerless. The first is the dotcom industry. The dotcom industries moved underclass and middle class people into the upper class. At the beginning of the Internet boom, millions of dollars could be earned in a single day. When Netscape, now the second largest Internet provider, did its initial public offering (IPO) in 1995, it earned $2 billion in just one day. A $12 million dollar investment turned into an $800 million profit. Venture capitalists immediately began to pour money into web start-up companies, hoping for similar results. Remember all the Superbowl commercials that year? It seemed as though every other commercial was for an Internet company. And the results for a time were phenomenal. As I said, people moved from lower or middle class to instant upper class as businesses moved out of their garages and into virtual space.

Many of these companies are going bankrupt now. Analysts say that the collapse of the dotcom industry will devastate the economy, and not just those who are on the front lines. It will also impact ad agencies, magazines and television programs that carry advertising, photographers, graphic designers, and web developers, as well as those who support those industries and services such as restaurants, book stores, car dealerships, etc. Go further and you find all those who supply services to them, such as cleaning services, food preparation services, and so forth. Many will suffer unemployment from the top on down.

So the Internet boom propelled people into the upper class and many of them are bypassing the middle class on their bankrupted way back down. Still, one important fact remains. The Internet changed the way business is done around the world.

Immigration, on the other hand, is bringing in large numbers of people to the underclass or poverty level. There's not a significant number moving from the underclass into middle class. "The reigning American mythology that being in a low-wage job is a temporary situation, that mobility will solve the problem, undermines such concern. But the evidence belies the myth. While some lower-wage workers will move up the ladder, most will never move into the middle class. Their children will suffer the same fate. Ignoring this reality leaves in place what Harvard economist Richard Freeman calls an 'apartheid economy.'"[7] The system is breaking down. The things that were meant to bring people to a higher standard of living, such as unions and workers' rights, have been or are being eliminated or successfully avoided. The better jobs, the middle class jobs, including high-tech jobs, are going overseas. The poor are remaining poor, and there's more and more of them.

With all the jobs that have moved overseas and the companies that have moved their operations, you'd think it would have bankrupted this country already. It would have. If the people at the Enmeshed extreme were waiting to find jobs in the United States, we'd be broke. But they're not waiting. They're setting up their own jobs and creating an underground economy.

## Entrepreneurs and the Underground Economy

It is difficult if not impossible to get accurate statistics on the number of people who are self-employed or who are running start-up companies. While we can gather statistics on those who apply for a business license or who buy a business name or location, such information doesn't take into account the number of people who simply do business without the required forms or formal structures. Further, it doesn't take into account the untaxed underground economy.

I don't think that we're going to get rid of the Individualistic extreme, but we are moving toward the Enmeshed extreme. And yet, as we saw in the last chapter on education, most of the preparation in schools and colleges is geared toward the Individualistic extreme. Not all entrepreneurships are going to grow into great corporations, however. Nor are all taco vendors going to own their own restaurants. There's always going to be the need for the smaller mom-and-pop shops.

Where does the entrepreneurial spirit lead the Latino population? We see a lot in the service industries, lawn service, house cleaning, food service. We actually see the Latino population following the Asian population. For example, the Asian population is highly concentrated in the medical field. If you go into communities where doctors live, very upscale communities, you'll see more Latinos in those communities taking care of the house, the lawn, and the cars, and doing maintenance and house painting. It makes sense to follow the Asian population.

We follow the Asians for jobs and the Italians for housing. In Denver you can track where the Latino population is moving by tracking the Italian population. North Denver used to be totally Italian, now it's totally Latino. You have the same kind of thing further west. Years ago, the only people who would sell their homes to Latinos were the Italians. Whites wouldn't sell homes to the Latinos because "there goes the neighborhood," and property values dropped. Italians would. I suggest that the way you can tell that the Mexicans are following the Italians is that the wrought iron fences get painted black. The Italians paint them white, and the Mexicans paint them black. It's my own way of doing demographic studies!

So Latinos follow Asians for work, Italians for housing. You can see these communities changing in those ways. Part of it is that the economy drives it. If the Asian population does well, so does the Latino population. We don't do it at the same level, but we are as effective. You have Mexican-owned janitorial firms that make as much money as those doctors make. We just have to clean thirty houses and mow thirty lawns, but we can make as much as the doctor makes by doing that.

Let's go back to the example of the man who wants to start a lawn-mowing business. He knows that he has the training to mow lawns. All he has to do is find the lawns. He doesn't have to go to college or even earn a high school diploma. All he has to do is purchase some equipment like three lawnmowers and a pickup truck in which he can haul everything. And he'll always be able to find help. It takes less than an hour to mow an average size lawn, so you can probably mow ten lawns a day. You can charge $25 a week to mow someone's lawn. It doesn't take much thought to realize that you can make more than the current $5.75 minimum wage.

I have a friend who serves as the perfect example. Being a true entrepreneur, he saw a need and filled it. He noticed that a lot of people either didn't know what to do with their appliances when they were getting rid of them or just put them out on the curb for trash removal. He started going to those people and for a small fee would remove the appliance for them. He would then fix the appliance and sell it to a second-hand store. He's just bought a brand new pick-up truck with the money he's made. Not many young men his age could afford the same truck when they're making minimum wage.

There is a lot of drive to do this. A lot of the kids of these immigrants are learning that entrepreneurial spirit at a young age. Certainly some of these kids will get an education and go on to do great things. I think they'll be stronger in many ways than the kids who have grown up on the Individualistic extreme. For the Enmeshed kids, they've seen what running a business takes. Most Individualistic kids don't learn that until they get to college. Sure, they see that dad gets up early and goes to work, but half of them don't even know what he does, as long as there's money to buy Air Jordans and cell phones. On the Enmeshed side, as soon as the kids are old enough, they're helping in the afternoons after school or washing dishes and taking care of their siblings. They have work experience by the time they hit high school.

It creates a lot of conflict when immigrants are seen as taking American jobs. Immigrants, though, see themselves as entitled to the American Dream. Native-born Americans don't necessarily see it that way. They might say, "Of course they're not entitled, they weren't born here." The immigrants, though, are saying, "If we work hard, we can make it here. It's not that difficult. So we'll do whatever it takes to make it. If I work three jobs, I work three jobs. If we need food stamps, we'll get food stamps. We'll work for cash." They are raising their kids with the attitude of "We're here, we have every right to be here, and we belong here."

That's why I'm suggesting that the kids growing up on the Enmeshed side might come out stronger than the kids growing up on the Individualistic side.

Another piece of this entrepreneurial puzzle is the underground economy that helps fuel our country. In the entrepreneurships, in the churro wars in California and the taco vendors in Denver, in the Arab newspapers in New

York, there lies a good deal of money. While some of the vendors may have papers and tax forms and licenses, many do not. Many don't pay an income tax. And yet, they are also the ones who will buy a big, shiny pick-up truck to show how well they have participated in the American Dream. What happens to our economy when these immigrants, many of them illegal, aren't allowed to cross the borders and so they stop buying our trucks and televisions, houses and apartments?

I have a brother who was selling a house in Denver. They sold the house, a family was approved for a loan, and they went to closing. Right before closing, the lender found out the people who were buying the house had illegal documents, so it fell apart. So here's a family with illegal documents, and they have enough money to buy a house, to get approved, and then get all the way to the closing. They would have closed had the false documents not been discovered.

I'm convinced that there are many out there not being discovered, who are illegal aliens but who are paying property taxes and own their own piece of the American dream. Or the illegal American Dream in this case. Their social security number, either legally or illegally obtained, had already gotten them through the credit checks. Not everybody gets caught. As long as they don't get into trouble, they'll probably never be questioned. They'll live here illegally. Once again, take that out of the economy, shift them all back to their own countries, and then who picks the fruit and cleans the toilets, and who buys the trucks and rents the apartments? It would destroy our already shaky economy. As Hansen said in *Mexifornia*, you're not going to get the kids hanging out at the mall to go and pick fruit on the farms. That's not going to happen.

The real question I think will be, how will this largely Latino population react once they move from the Enmeshed side to the Individualistic side? Will they care any more for the powerless? I'm not convinced that they'll care for this group any more than anybody else has, but I am convinced that they'll care more about Latin American interests. I foresee many more corporate partnerships with Latin America and Mexico. We'll always have the poor in this country, because the colonized will become the colonizer. But I think the economy of Latin American countries will be much improved.

If we can improve the economy and financial state of Latinos and other minorities in this country, we will all be much improved as well.

## The Underemployed

The majority of low-wage jobs fall to women, minorities, and immigrants. America seems to be indifferent to these invisible workers, these workers who take care of our parents, serve our food, and clean our houses.

> Much public attention is focused on moving Americans off of welfare, and almost everywhere, it seems, there have been calls to ensure that those who receive government welfare assistance perform work. But little outrage is reserved for the over thirty million Americans who work hard every day, and yet struggle to take care of their families. Who these workers are contributes to this public indifference. A majority are female and many are minorities and immigrants. These groups historically have been forgotten, viewed as somehow less deserving or less in need of support. It is

135

only with the plunging wages of working-class white males that some attention has been paid.[8]

Alan Webber notes that the plunging wages of white males may have a political impact as well. White males are traditionally Republican; working class females and minorities lean to the Democratic party. And President Bush has done something to help these plunging wages by pledging to appoint an assistant secretary of Commerce for manufacturing. These are the statistics he quotes: "The country has lost 3 million jobs over the past three years, 2.5 million of them in manufacturing. One survey found that 18% of American workers reported being laid off in the past three years. And this summer the average length of unemployment jumped to 19 weeks, the highest level in 20 years." The most concern is expressed over middle-aged white men who have lost middle-income jobs. "As a consequence, there's a whole cross-section of middle-aged American men who are angry and bitter. They don't know how their final 10 years in the workforce will play out. Their old jobs are gone. They can't find new ones. And nobody seems to be paying much attention to the problem. They are feeling left out and betrayed." And it's not just middle-aged men, Webber states. It's also young men in their 20s who don't have much to hope for beyond low-paying jobs.[9]

An African-American woman wrote into the editor with the terse comment, "Welcome to the club." Men and women of color and white women have felt displaced, betrayed, underpaid, angry, and bitter for as long as this country has been around. And nobody, as Webber wrongly stated about white men, seems to be paying much attention to the problem.

Much more could be said about this problem, and entire books have been devoted to it. Let me finish this section with Shulman's challenge:

> Why should we care that over thirty million Americans and their families face these conditions? We should care because it is morally repugnant. In a nation as rich as ours, where CEOs make four hundred times the average rank-and-file worker, leaving workers without the basic protections of life should be unthinkable. While one can argue that certain individuals should receive larger rewards than others for their contributions in society, it is quite another story to leave those who have worked hard without even the minimal necessities.[10]

## But What About Marketing?

It would be odd in a chapter on business to not talk about marketing and advertising, the very force that drives business. I want to offer a few words here regarding marketing and how businesses are beginning to feel the effect of a larger Latino population; however, the greater part of my discussion of marketing will be taken up in chapter 7.

Harvey Mackay takes note of the expanding Latino population and asks, what should business people be doing? They should make ads and packaging in both English and Spanish. "About 68 percent of U.S. Hispanics speak Spanish at home. That's not to be taken lightly if you're selling potato chips or toothpaste."[11] However, it's not enough to just translate what you have into Spanish. You must understand to a certain degree the people and the culture. "'It's not just translating from Spanish to English,' says [Luis] Maizel. "The concept of family and trust is different. Companies need to experience life. They need an interpreter, not of language, but of culture.'"[12]

A good example of this was a targeted ad campaign used by the Las Vegas Convention and Visitors Authority that marketed Las Vegas to Latinos. President of the advertising company, Mary Ann Mele said that the campaign was "more literal and more product-oriented. The TV spots show extended families in specific situations such as dining and dancing and winning at the slots." Chrysanthe Georges, a consultant on marketing to the Latino community, liked the ads and said, "The biggest thing is to be culturally attuned . . . And that means you just can't translate your pitch from English to Spanish . . . It's a more emotional culture."[13] Remember that touchy-feely culture we talked about in education? Here it is in marketing. It's all about relationships.

Further, know your market. Don't assume that Latinos are all one market. They come from Mexico, Cuba, Puerto Rico, Spain, and South and Central America. They are as different, he notes, as Maine and Texas. Have Latinos look over your products, ads, and packaging, as well as recruiting Latinos in key positions in your company.[14]

For example, the San Diego Padres baseball team hired Enrique Morones in 1995 to head its newly created Hispanic marketing division. They saw the Hispanic fan base grow from 50,000 to more than 600,000 through such strategies as recognizing Mother's Day in Mexico and handing out flowers to moms who attended the game, and opening Padres' stores and ticket outlets in Tijuana, Mexico. Morones, who is no longer with the Padres, said, "Token events won't work. People need to see a concentrated effort on the part of any company. They need to see Latinos as department heads – not just someone with a Hispanic surname – and they want to see the company taking an active role in the community."[15]

Another company taking the Latino opportunity seriously is burrito restaurant Chipotle. "Often in restaurants, non-English-speaking employees are relegated to the kitchen or work busing tables, hindered by a lack of language skills from reaching higher-paying jobs that require more customer contact."[16] So Chipotle offers a program to workers to learn English as a tool for moving up in the company. Classes are done in the stores, and employees are paid their regular wages for attending. More than just teaching English, though, the classes also help translate the cultural differences.

And isn't that part of the exciting changes occurring in our country, translating culture?

## Questions for Reflection

What about a barter economy?
Can we flatten the hierarchical system?
Who is buying and who is selling in the future?

## Summary: Business on the Model

The Individualistic extreme views business as "bigger is better." Corporations will compete for bigger market shares, higher profits, and higher salaries. They typically offer benefits packages that include retirement and health. Corporations are defined by vision, mission statements, and 5-year plans. People at the Individualistic extreme believe they are entitled to the American Dream because they were born here.

The Enmeshed extreme works for significance and customer loyalty. They work for what they need and see no reason to work beyond that. Their structure is simple, often uni-layered or owned by one person. Often they don't have retirement plans or health benefits, believing that once they reach a certain age, they will just hire younger people to keep the business going. People at the Enmeshed extreme are convinced they are entitled to the American Dream because they came here believing that America is the land of opportunity.

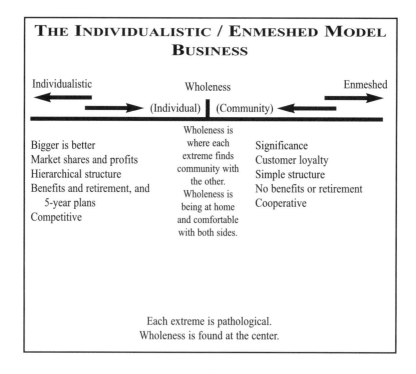

## THE INDIVIDUALISTIC / ENMESHED MODEL BUSINESS

Individualistic       Wholeness       Enmeshed

(Individual) | (Community)

Bigger is better
Market shares and profits
Hierarchical structure
Benefits and retirement, and
   5-year plans
Competitive

Wholeness is where each extreme finds community with the other. Wholeness is being at home and comfortable with both sides.

Significance
Customer loyalty
Simple structure
No benefits or retirement
Cooperative

Each extreme is pathological.
Wholeness is found at the center.

# Notes

[1] Mort Zuckerman, "All Work and No Play," *US News & World Report*, Sep 8, 2003.

[2] See Chapter 9 of this book.

[3] Louis Uchitelle, "A Missing Statistic: U.S. Jobs That Went Overseas," *New York Times*, Oct. 5, 2003.

[4] Uchitelle, "A Missing Statistic."

[5] As reported on Howard Dean's website, www.deanforamerica.com, excerpted from labornews.com.

[6] Uchitelle, "A Missing Statistic."

[7] Beth Shulman, *The Betrayal of Work: How Low-Wage Jobs Fail 30 Million Americans* (New York: The New York Press, 2003), 7.

[8] Ibid.

[9] Alan M. Webber, "Beware of Angry, Jobless Men," *USA Today*, Sep. 7, 2003.

[10] Shulman, *The Betrayal of Work*, 81.

[11] Harvey Mackay, "Are You Ready to Ride that Hispanic Wave?" *The Denver Post*, Aug. 19, 2001, 12K.

[12] Laura Castaneda, "Getting a Piece of the Flan: Smart Marketing, Not Just Good Products, Is Needed to Earn a Piece of the $452 Billion Hispanic Market," *San Diego Metropolitan*, July 2002.

[13] Ian Mylchreest, "Minorities Need More Than Just Translating," *Hispanic Business,* Oct. 27, 2003.

[14] Mackay, " Hispanic Wave?"

[15] Castaneda, "Getting a Piece of the Flan."

[16] Janet Forgrieve, "Talking the Talk: Chipotle Gives Hispanic Workers English Lessons, Chance to Move Ahead," *Rocky Mountain News*, Sep. 27, 2003.

# Chapter 6

## The Justice System: Blind Balances?

I pledge allegiance to the flag of the United States of America, and to the Republic for which it stands, one nation under God, indivisible, with liberty and justice for all." It may have been years since you've said the Pledge of Allegiance. I know for me, it hasn't been since I was in school. When I was in school, though, I said it every day, standing up and facing the flag, my right hand over my heart, the words ringing out from the classmates around me.

We could, of course, get into a lengthy discussion on the troublesome phrase "under God." After all, if I'm a Christian, isn't that the phrase I want to protect? What I would like to do in this chapter, however, is focus on a more troubling, and oftentimes overlooked, phrase: "and justice for all." Whether or not there is truly justice for all in this country, and how our justice system fits the model are subjects this chapter will attempt to illuminate.

## Justice: An Overview

It's difficult to look at some of the statistics on crime and the justice system and not see racism. It might well be impossible. Consider that, for example, according to the Substance Abuse and Mental Health Services Administration, National Household Survey on Drug Abuse, most illicit drug users, approximately 72 percent, are white, 15 percent are black, and 10 percent are Hispanic. And yet, of those in state prisons for drug felonies, 58 percent are African Americans, and 20.7 percent are Hispanic.[1] That's quite a reverse pyramid. In fact, according to the Human Rights Watch, "In no state are black men incarcerated at rates even close to those of white men. Nationwide, black men are incarcerated at 9.6 times the rate of white men. In eleven states, black men are incarcerated at rates that are twelve to twenty-six times greater than those of white men."[2] The rates for black and white drug offenses reveal that blacks on average are thirteen times more likely to be incarcerated.

The "war on drugs" has created overcrowded prisons for crimes that are non-violent. Retired General Barry McCaffrey, director of the Office of National Drug Control Policy, states that "drug control policies bear primary responsibility for the quadrupling of the national prison population since 1980 and a soaring incarceration rate, the highest among western democracies." And yet, as Human Rights Watch noted, we sometimes forget that prison is meant to be the harshest punishment, short of death, that our justice system can mete out. "Short of executions, imprisonment is the most severe exercise of a government's legitimate coercive and penal powers." But if the system is routinely sweeping the streets and incarcerating large numbers of African-American men for non-violent crimes, taking away their right to citizenship through the vote, where is the justice? The solution is "to reduce the use of prison for low-level drug offenders and to increase the availability of substance abuse treatment."[3]

While the statistics mentioned above were for adult prisoners, racial disparity is seen in the sentencing of youth as well. According to Amnesty International in 1998, "African-American youths constitute only 15% of the population between the ages of 10 and 17, 30% of the youths arrested, 40% of those held in custody, and 50% of those who are transferred to stand trial as adults in criminal court are African-American." Oftentimes, particularly in these days of believing that the young should be treated as adults, these young offenders are placed in facilities with adult offenders where they face sexual molestation, physical abuse, higher rates of suicide, and lower rates of rehabilitation.

Racial disparity is also evident in cases where the death penalty is sought. Between 1995-2000, in cases where the death penalty was sought, 80 percent of the defendants were minorities. The race of the murder victim has also been a factor. Prosecutors were almost twice as likely to seek the death penalty for a black defendant when the victim was non-black (20 percent if the victim was black compared to 36 percent if the victim was non-black). Correspondingly, when prosecutors were seeking the death penalty for a white defendant, the percentage actually went down if the victim wasn't white, with the death penalty sought 38 percent of the time when the victim was white compared to 35 percent when the victim was not white. Apparently, a black life isn't worth as much as a white one.

In the same time period of 1995-2000, the Attorney General of the United States authorized seeking the death penalty in 159 cases. Of those, 51 cases entered into plea agreements (an agreement that results in a guilty plea for a lesser sentence). The racial breakdown is staggering. Of those 51, 48 percent were white (21 out of 44), 25 percent black (18 out of 71), 28 percent Hispanic (9 out of 32), and 25 percent other (3 out of 12). It is possible that race plays an indirect rather than direct hand in the plea bargain statistics, as whites are more likely to have hired private counsel.[4]

These statistics are devastating to the black population. One in every twenty black men over 18 is in state or federal prison. This impacts several areas. First, the family. Fifty-six percent of the prison population are parents. We've seen in the family chapter how single-parent families are the new poor. Second, and this is linked to the family, is that ex-cons have a harder time finding a job when they get out of prison, and if they do, they generally make a good deal less money than do others. What ever happened to "paying one's debt to society"? Apparently, the debt never ends. And when jobs are hard to find and the family is hungry, the temptation to return to crime and the lure of easy money is high. Third, racial disparity in the justice system impacts politics and fair representation in our country. Almost 1.5 million African-American men out of a total voting population of 10.4 million have lost their right to vote due to felony convictions. The powerful get more powerful and the powerless get more oppressed.

## Some High-Profile Cases

It certainly looks as though racism is alive, well, and rampant in the criminal justice system. I would like, though, to go back to what I brought up in chapter 2. I don't think it's so much a problem of race as it is with whether you are powerful or powerless, Individualistic or Enmeshed. Traditionally, the people on the powerless side have been people of color, so we tend to equate powerlessness with race. However, when you look at the statistics, it's not wealthy blacks who are in prison. Race isn't on the model.

This country's justice system is based on a

powerful/powerless structure and has a mindset that esteems "success." It's a system that, while claiming to be impartial, says, if you are poor, addicted to drugs, and get caught, you go to jail. But if you are Rush Limbaugh, addicted to drugs, and get caught, you get to keep your radio show and go to rehab. We can't even count how many times Robert Downey, Jr., a white actor, has been given a "second chance" in the land of "three strikes, you're out."

In order to see the powerful/powerless structure, I want to consider three separate crime stories to see how both sides looked at it.

## O.J. Simpson

The O.J. Simpson trial was a defining moment for this country. Simpson, who had been in jail during his murder trial, was acquitted in October 1995 in the deaths of his ex-wife Nicole Brown Simpson and her friend Ron Goldman.

In a civil suit that followed in 1996, CNN reported that the pool of prospective jurors had split along racial lines. Whites were saying that Simpson probably was guilty of (and had gotten away with) murder; African Americans were saying that Simpson was innocent. For example, consider these three jurors in the prospective pool:

> \* A white woman who said it could be a struggle for her to overcome her preconceived notion that Simpson is a wife batterer and double-murderer. . . . Judge Hiroshi Fujisaki told her to come back for the final phase of jury selection.
> \* A white man who compared expert witnesses, including Simpson's own star scientist Henry Lee, with prostitutes who'll say and do anything for money. The man

said he was inclined to believe Simpson is guilty.

* A black man who said he tended to believe Simpson was innocent, that the Los Angeles Police Department "jumped to conclusions" in suspecting Simpson early on, and that there was "something wrong" with the evidence.[5]

The first prospective juror admitted to a preconceived bias, and this about a man who had been acquitted of murder. She admitted that she couldn't believe "innocent until proven guilty." The second one believed Simpson to be guilty based on the powerful/powerless structure. Simpson was probably guilty but got acquitted, because he was able to hire enough expert witnesses and lawyers who would lie for money. The third one is representative of a lot of African Americans who have trouble trusting the police, and who believe that the police tried to frame Simpson by tampering with the evidence. In fact, many people feel that police officer Mark Fuhrman's racist attitudes did little to help the prosecution, and confirmed what many African Americans feel, that the police are not to be trusted.

Regarding the second juror, that opinion was a majority one in the criminal trial. In a CNN/USA Today-Gallup Poll conducted on Oct. 3, 1995, 639 people were asked whether Simpson's wealth played a key role in getting a not guilty verdict because Simpson could afford the best legal advice available. A whopping 73 percent believed that he would have been convicted if he had not been wealthy. In the same poll, people were asked if race had any effect upon the jury. Thirty-four percent believed that racial issues determined the verdict, and thirty-eight percent believed that racial issues were considered by the jury as they related to other evidence. Only 22 percent believed that race played no part in the verdict.

And these opinions weren't held just in America. British ITN Deputy Editor Michael Jermey said, "I think a lot of people have looked at American society through the prism of the O.J. Simpson case, seen the racial divisions, seen the issues of access to the judicial system been helped by extreme wealth, and perhaps conclusions have been drawn about the American social system."[6]

The reactions to the O.J. Simpson trial highlight the issue of power and wealth at the Individualistic extreme. Again, the Pledge of Allegiance states "and justice for all."

And yet, the quality of that justice seems to be for sale to the highest bidder. Let's say a poor person is brought to trial and is given a public defender, and a wealthy person is brought to trial and brings with him his own personal lawyers. It doesn't take a legal genius to know which one is going to get the better defense.

> The structure of the legal profession and the way that it functions also produces deleterious effects. Minorities and women are underrepresented not only in law schools, but among the ranks of practicing attorneys. The best attorneys from the best law schools most often secure employment with prestigious law firms practicing highly lucrative civil and corporate law. The net effect has been an erosion in the quality of criminal defense attorneys. Studies of public defenders and court appointed attorneys show that the type of legal assistance provided by them to indigent defendants is qualitatively different from that provided by retained counsel. Judges are selected from

the highest strata of the legal profession. Together, these factors produce a situation where there are few similarities between criminal defendants and those who occupy critical positions in the legal system.[7]

In the CNN poll, 73 percent of Americans believed that wealth was an issue in the case. It's not my intention here to argue either that O.J. Simpson was guilty and got off or was (and is) innocent. My intention is to point out that on the Individualistic/Enmeshed model, those who are successful and powerful have access to things that the powerless do not. "Justice for all" is taking a beating.

## Kobe Bryant

The current and still occurring trial of Los Angeles Lakers' basketball star Kobe Bryant gives us a more updated look at the issue. Bryant was accused of raping a nineteen-year-old woman. He says the act was consensual. Again, as with the Simpson case, the point for this purpose of this book is not to rehash evidence and decide guilt or innocence. The issue, which is being ignored by the media as well as by the court system, is one of power.

Early news stories focused on Bryant's "affair" and showed pictures of him with his beautiful – and forgiving – wife. Popular opinion was that this young woman was "miffed" for some reason and accused Bryant of rape. Stories ranged that she had perhaps tried to get money and had been refused, or that perhaps she was disappointed that he had no plans to leave his wife for her, or that she had just been disappointed that the sex was over so quickly and had not been emotionally intimate. Sympathy, always hard to come by in a rape trial, was definitely with Bryant, who had shown bad judgment and a certain lack of moral certitude, but had not raped anyone.

While our justice system is based on "innocent until proven guilty" – a noble and important sentiment – innocence in this case has not been granted to Bryant on such a lofty ideal. Innocence in this case has been granted based on celebrity, based on the Individualistic power that Bryant holds.

One of the statements that kept being repeated during the early days of Bryant's alleged crime was "it couldn't be him; he just wouldn't do that." He's one of the nice guys – the well-respected, successful, talented, famous nice guys. Because of that "nice guy" image, the media overlooked the fact that he lied about having sex with the woman to begin with. When he couldn't lie about it any more, he then admitted that he had had sex, but claimed that it was consensual.

The victim, who will not be named in this book although her name is known, is powerless, at the Enmeshed extreme. First, Tom Leykis, the shock-jock host of a radio talk-show based in Los Angeles, began using the woman's name on the air. Then *The Globe* published a picture of her on their cover along with her name – something that is avoided in rape cases due to the nature of rape. *The Globe* said that if she's going to file charges, people should know who she is. The picture is allegedly a prom picture. She's dressed in white, but is hiking up her skirt to reveal a good deal of thigh and a garter. It looks like she's dressed in lingerie. She certainly doesn't look like a victim. It's one of the trashiest pictures I've ever seen, but not because of how she looks. It's trashy, because what we're seeing is the trashing of the powerless by the powerful, in this case by sports fans, the media, and the cult of the celebrity.

One of the outcomes of having her accuse a "star" is that she has received death threats, and Bryant received an offer from someone to kill the woman. In how many rape cases does that occur? Only in the high-profile ones.

I said that Bryant's accuser doesn't look like a victim. She certainly doesn't look like how we want our victims to look. But in actuality, how do victims of rape look? They look like mothers, grandmothers, sisters, daughters, wives. They are of all ages, all races, all religions, all genders. Another story that was published about this woman was her alleged drug use and possible overdose a week before she accused Bryant. While it is standard practice for lawyers to attack the background of a witness in order to establish reasonable doubt, this was reported so lasciviously by journalists as to call their motives into question. Further, Colorado's Rape Shield Law prevents attacking the victim's character and sexual history, which was allowed at the preliminary hearing.

This is a clear case of seeing the Individualistic person as "one of us" and the Enmeshed person as "one of them." In this particular case, the powerful person is an African American.

## JonBenet Ramsey

On Dec. 26, 1996, six-year-old JonBenet Ramsey, whom people believed to have been kidnapped, was found murdered in her home in Boulder, Colorado. Over subsequent days, the media revealed photos of her that fueled suspicions that her parents had something to do with the crime. The photos showed JonBenet, the beauty contestant, wearing costumes that at times were too mature for a six year old. Stories were circulated about the appropriateness of such contests for young girls, and questions were raised about the suitableness of such parents.

The point I want to make is that today, seven years later, we're still hearing about JonBenet. E! Entertainment recently ran a "True Hollywood Story" episode on the crime. The *Rocky Mountain News* still carries links to their stories about JonBenet Ramsey as well as stories about the Columbine killings, 9-11, and the bombing in Oklahoma City. Mike Littwin, a columnist for the *Rocky Mountain News*, wrote, "At some point, actually very quickly, the story became a soap opera – think O.J. in tights – and the soap opera long ago became more important than the actual crime."[8]

I am not suggesting by any means that we shouldn't consider JonBenet Ramsey's death a tragic one. But adding to the tragedy is the fact that children all over the country are murdered, and we don't remember their names. We haven't hung on every word of the district attorneys as they've tried to solve these other cases. We haven't demanded the firing of the police officers that we believe mishandled the case. Once the initial reporting is done, we don't hear anything further on the news or on entertainment shows.

Certainly, murders in Boulder, Colorado, are rarer than murders in Denver or any other large metropolis. True, police officers in Boulder may have bungled things because they're not used to dealing with the violent crimes that large city officers deal with daily. But the media parade doesn't make darlings out of poor children or out of children of color. Most murder victims aren't rich and don't dress in cute little outfits. Is it too harsh to say, "What's the death of one more poor kid"?

In writing about the Ramseys, Littwin said:

> Sometimes it looks as if the Ramseys do everything they can to make themselves look guilty. From the start, when they hired lawyers and refused to cooperate with the police, they courted suspicion. The runway video, and the idea of little JonBenet

vamping in those ugly beauty contests, made the Ramseys look, at the very least, unsympathetic. I'm not making the case for their innocence or guilt. I don't even have an opinion. *My opinion is that rich people have a better chance of getting away with murder than poor people.* And that, conversely, if the Ramseys weren't rich, . . . JonBenet would have long ago slipped into distant memory.[9]

# A Troubling Question

A recent crime in Denver brought some of these questions to light. On July 5, 2003, police received a 911 call for a family disturbance. Fifteen-year-old Paul Childs was threatening his family with a knife. When police arrived, Childs had the knife on him, and police officer James Turney shot and killed him. It was later revealed that Childs, an African American, was developmentally disabled, and that Turney a year and a half earlier had killed in the line of duty a hearing-impaired African-American teenager. While there was much speculation about the knife, the level of threat, and how often the Childs' family had called for police intervention, many people feel that the police were too quick to open fire. The former president of the African-American Ministerial Association, Rev. Patrick Demmer, who attended a vigil calling for an independent investigation of the shooting, said, "Had that been a wild bear or a mountain lion, they would have tranquilized him. . . . We have to have justice. Something is wrong with our system."[10]

Denver District Attorney Bill Ritter investigated the shooting and came to the conclusion that the officer acted appropriately and would not be charged. Bill Johnson, a columnist with the *Rocky Mountain News*, wrote that he would have bet money on that decision, because Ritter has never brought charges in the seventy or so officer-involved shootings that have occurred on his watch. Johnson, this time though, agreed with the ruling. Ritter, he says, would never be able to make the charges stick.

Less than a week after his column ran, Johnson attended a protest march demanding justice and offering support for Childs' family. At the march, he met 72-year-old Catherine Bryant who was attending her first protest. He summarized her message: "We as citizens have a duty to let not only the mayor and the police chief know, but let everyone know what happened to that developmentally disabled 15-year-old was unnecessary and outrageous."

But the real moment for Johnson, and for those concerned for the powerless in our country, came when they were saying their good-byes. Bryant asked Johnson if he had a son. She asked, "If he were so out of line today that you needed the police, would you call?"[11]

He said that his answer still stuns him. Johnson is well educated and comfortable with the system, but when the question is asked, he's not comfortable with what his gut tells him. Even for middle-class people, it raises the question, would you call? The implications should stun all of us. When did the police become not those who are sworn to protect and defend, but instead those whom we fear? For the Enmeshed, for the powerless, this is who the police have always been.

Add to this public perception the fact of racial profiling. Profiling, according to reason.com, is "the practice of stopping and inspecting people who are passing through public places – such as drivers on public highways or pedestrians in airports or urban areas – where the reason for the stop is a statistical profile of the detainee's race or ethnicity." It is investigating people before any crime has been committed, based simply on race. Some defend the practice as being practical and necessary. John Derbyshire of National Review wrote, "A policeman who concentrates a disproportionate amount of his limited time and resources on young black men is going to uncover far more crimes – and therefore be far more successful in his career – than one who biases his attention toward, say, middle-aged Asian women."[12] Is it any wonder that African Americans don't trust the police?

David Barstow wrote in the New York Times about a neighborhood in Brooklyn. "'Almost every black or Hispanic teen-ager on the street has a story of being stopped and frisked, often several times a month, sometimes in the lobbies of their own apartment buildings.' Said a teen-ager in another neighborhood, 'We always fit the description.'"[13]

My youngest son, Jerome, has a similar story. Glenda and I decided when we bought a new car to give our old one, a BMW, to Jerome. He would go out every week with the youth group he was involved in, and he was thrilled to have a car to chaperone his friends. One night, I watched as the car drove up and saw that one of Jerome's friends, a white boy, was driving the car. I asked Jerome about it. I mean, he was so thrilled to have the car, so why wasn't he the one driving it? He told me that every time he drove, the police stopped him, wanting to make sure that the BMW was registered to him. His white friend, on the other hand, never got stopped. For Jerome, it was just easier to let his friend drive.

This sad state should anger every American for it violates the Pledge of Allegiance's "and justice for all," not to mention several Constitutional rights.

While profiling has been used for quite some time against African Americans and Latinos in the drug war, it has been on the rise in these post-September 11 days against those of Arab descent. I recently asked a Christian group a troubling question. What are we going to do in this country about Christian terrorists? The group was shocked. What Christian terrorists?

Don't you find it interesting that after Timothy McVeigh blew up the Federal Building in Oklahoma City, the attorney general of the United States didn't pick up every skinhead in the country and send them to Guantanamo Bay? After all, isn't that where the Arab detainees are? McVeigh claimed to be a Christian. The Aryan Nation does these kinds of terrorist acts in the name of Christ. So why aren't we rounding up Christians? Because, we say, people like McVeigh are not really Christians; they're a crazy fringe group. Unfortunately, we won't let Muslims say the same. We insist that all Muslims are fundamentalist extremists who will kill us if given half a chance. They're trying to tell us that they have crazies too, but we won't listen. So again, what are we going to do with Christian terrorists?

All of us should feel a bit uncomfortable at that kind of double standard when it comes to "justice."

## Questions for Reflection

Can we imprison all those who disagree with us?

How does jailing the poor make us all poorer?

Should we change the Pledge of Allegiance to read "justice for some"?

157

# Summary: Justice on the Model

The Individualistic extreme enjoys the benefits of being powerful. They have better attorneys and so have the ability to plea bargain down to lesser crimes, often with no jail time. Because they also have a greater ability to post bail, the time they are incarcerated is greatly reduced. Even when they aren't innocent, though, this powerful extreme has lower percentages for incarceration, sentencing, and death penalties. The Individualistic extreme views the police as protectors, both of property and life, and defenders against crime.

The Enmeshed extreme faces the realities of being powerless in America. They are the recipients of unjust racial and class profiling. When arrested, because they often

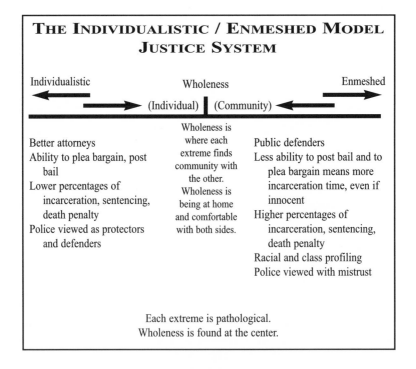

**THE INDIVIDUALISTIC / ENMESHED MODEL JUSTICE SYSTEM**

Individualistic | Wholeness | Enmeshed

(Individual) | (Community)

| Individualistic | Wholeness | Enmeshed |
|---|---|---|
| Better attorneys | Wholeness is where each extreme finds community with the other. Wholeness is being at home and comfortable with both sides. | Public defenders |
| Ability to plea bargain, post bail | | Less ability to post bail and to plea bargain means more incarceration time, even if innocent |
| Lower percentages of incarceration, sentencing, death penalty | | Higher percentages of incarceration, sentencing, death penalty |
| Police viewed as protectors and defenders | | Racial and class profiling |
| | | Police viewed with mistrust |

Each extreme is pathological.
Wholeness is found at the center.

don't have the ability to post bail, they spend higher amounts of time in jail – even when they are innocent. Again, because they cannot hire the best attorneys and must rely on public defenders, they have higher percentages of incarceration, sentencing, and death penalties. Because of these things, the Enmeshed extreme view the police with mistrust, not as protectors but as persecutors.

## Notes

[1] Quoted on Drug War Facts: Race, Prison and the Drug Laws, www.drugwarfacts.org/racepris.htm.

[2] http://www.hrw.org/campaigns/drugs/war/adult-male.htm

[3] *Human Rights Watch Report*, June 2000.

[4] These statistics were taken from *The Federal Death Penalty System: A Statistical Survey* (1988-2000).

[5] "Simpson Judge OKs Jury Prospects Who Admit Bias," *CNN*, Sep. 25, 1996.

[6] Rob Reynolds, "'What a Farce': Simpson Trial Draws Jeers 'Round the World," *CNN*, Oct. 3, 1995.

[7] Victor E. Kappeler, Mark Blumberg, and Gary W. Potter, *The Mythology of Crime and Criminal Justice* (Prospect Heights, IL: Waveland Press, Inc., 1996). From the summary of Chapter 11: "Order in the Courts: The Myth of Equal Justice."

[8] Mike Littwin, "If Smit Is Right, What Does That Make Us?" *Rocky Mountain News*, May 5, 2001.

[9] Ibid. Emphasis mine.

[10] Lynn Bartels, "Remembering Teen, Demanding Justice," *Rocky Mountain News*, July 10, 2003.

[11] Bill Johnson, "Protester Pushed Me to a Place I Didn't Want to Go," *Rocky Mountain News*, October 22, 2003. See

also "A Gut-Wrenching, but Correct Decision," *Rocky Mountain News,* October 17, 2003.

[12] Quoted in reason.com, August-September 2001, http://reason.com/0108/fe.gc.the.shtml

[13] Quoted by Nat Hentoff, "Crime's Down, But Arrests Keep Rising," *Jewish World Review*, April 17, 2000.

# Chapter 7

## Entertainment and Marketing: Giving the People What They Want

You may wonder why I've chosen to deal with marketing and advertising in the entertainment chapter. I hope it will become clear by the end of the chapter how close these two seemingly separate concepts are and how they mold each other and, subsequently, mold American society.

There is no doubt that the changing demographics are changing the way we view popular culture, including books, movies, music, and television. Let's look at books for a moment. While some people may be familiar with the works of Gabriel Garcia Marquez, Latino authors have not been a major niche until recently.

> Not only are Latinos the fastest-growing minority in the United States, but authors with Spanish surnames also have become one of the nation's hottest literary commodities. Publisher HarperCollins launched a Latino imprint in 2001. New York agents have started to recruit Latino

authors; two new national book clubs specialize in Spanish-language books; and 2003 was designated "The Year of Publishing Latino Voices for America" by the American Association of Publishers.[1]

Before long, what Toni Morrison and Terry McMillan did for the African-American literature community and what Amy Tan did for the Asian community will be done by certain Latino authors such as Isabel Allende, Alisa Valdes-Rodriguez, Eric Garcia, and Richard Rodriguez. These authors will be more than just required reading in multicultural studies at the local college. They will move into mainstream literature, appear on bestsellers lists, and be adapted into movies.

And while this acceptance of minority groups in creative endeavors is happening in American popular culture, it isn't limited to America. Consider this perspective about J.K. Rowling's monstrously popular work, Harry Potter:

> Rowling carefully introduces crucial features of modern liberal Britain. The student body at Hogwarts is notably heterogeneous: Its houses hold a conspicuous mix of black, South Asian, Celtic, and Anglo-Saxon students. Girls are fully the equals of boys, as students, faculty, and Quidditch players. Most important, those who attend the prestigious school are drawn from rich and poor, privileged and obscure, urban and rural backgrounds. All accents are spoken at Hogwarts. . . . the school also exemplifies the progressive spirit of the new multi-ethnic, feminist,

democratic, postimperial, and communitarian U.K.[2]

Television lags behind this book culture, but it shows signs of changing. In June, a UCLA study was released that revealed that although Latinos are the largest minority in the United States, they comprise only 3 percent of the characters on primetime television. African Americans make up 16 percent, while the largest percentage, 69 percent, is white. Perhaps more troubling is the fact that the portrayal of Latinos is rarely positive. In a speech to MANA de Albuquerque, former FCC commissioner (1997-2001) Gloria Tristani said,

> The bad news is that Hispanic youth rarely see anyone on television who looks like them. . . . This is a problem. Studies demonstrate that young people feel it is important to see people who look like them on TV. Children want to identify with television characters, but it's hard to when no one looks like you. This is particularly true for Latinas. If a young Latina had watched every single prime time broadcast television show last year, she would have seen Latinas in only 5 of 902 recurring characters last season, and three out of those five characters worked in low level service jobs. One young Latina commented that "they never show us as being good people, having a career, going to school."[3]

The recent series "George Lopez," about a middle-class Latino man and his family, may prove to be another "Roseanne." If so, it gives a more positive portrayal of

Latinos than do certain shows which portray Latinos primarily as criminals. Now in its third season, "George Lopez" draws a successful ten million viewers each week and is currently the anchor of ABC's family-friendly Friday line-up.

Movies may provide more positive images of Latinos than does television. The success of director Robert Rodriguez highlights this. As the director of such critically acclaimed and highly popular films as the *Spy Kids* franchise as well as the *Desperado* series, Rodriguez headed the list of "25 Most Powerful Hispanics in Hollywood," published by *Hispanic Magazine* in April of 1996, and ranked 80th in *Premiere* magazine's 2003 annual "Power 100" list. Rodriguez is also known for his highly creative, and highly controlled, style, in which he acts as producer, director, writer, editor, and composer. His book *Rebel without a Crew: How a 23-Year-Old Film-maker Made a $7000 Movie and Became a Hollywood Player* includes a section entitled "Robert Rodriguez's 10 minute film school" and has become a staple for the next generation of filmmakers. (This is also an "extra" on the DVD for *Once Upon a Time in Mexico*.) Through his movies, Latino film stars such as Antonio Banderas and Salma Hayek have become household names.

In many ways, cultural diversity isn't an issue in music. For example, hip-hop music is a melding of black and Latin cultures in New York, but the majority of those who purchase or download hip-hop are white suburban kids. I know, because my eleven-year-old granddaughter is one of them!

Crossing over from music to movies and back again are such media stars as Jennifer Lopez, who gives us an interesting example of the Individualistic/Enmeshed model. While it may be debatable, Lopez gives every appearance of having grown up on the powerless, Enmeshed side. She was born and raised in the Bronx to middle class, Puerto Rican parents. At times embarrassed by her successes, she constantly refers to her less-than-glamorous upbringing, and makes statements that she's really just like everybody else. She's still "Jenny from the block." For those on the powerless side, however, it's hard to picture her as "one of us." Lopez is consistently on "most beautiful (or sexiest) people" lists and to date has made more money than many actresses, certainly more than any other Latina actress. She became the third actress to enter the $20 million club (following Julia Roberts and Cameron Diaz). Her estate in Florida is worth over $9 million. She has opened restaurants, has a clothing line and a perfume. If anyone should be on the powerful Individualistic side, it is Lopez.

So which is she – Enmeshed or Individualistic? Actually, Lopez is seen as flaky by both sides. Neither side will say that she's like us, neither the Enmeshed, which is where she came from, nor the Individualistic, which is where she is now. Neither extreme will claim her. The highly Individualistic side isn't ready to buy into Lopez' being there. She's a corporate success, but corporate leaders would never invite her to a serious corporate discussion. Yet she is very intelligent in marketing and all the activities she is undertaking. Madonna may be the only singer/actress with more business savvy. Lopez has marketed herself well, in her products, her clothing, and her choice of roles (well, maybe not *Gigli*).

The problem with making a shift from one side to the other is a lack of understanding both sides. It doesn't fit, unless they understand the significant differences between the two places. I don't think Lopez understands that. If she understood the differences, she wouldn't make ridiculous statements such as, "I'm just like everybody else." She's not just like everybody else, and everybody else knows that.

To see an example on the other extreme, look at someone like Alec Baldwin, whom many think may one day enter the political arena. Mark Weinberg, press secretary to former president Ronald Reagan, said, "There's a passion and maybe even an anger about some of the things that are wrong in this country – the disparity between the haves and have-nots. He gets angry and morally outraged when the government doesn't meet its responsibilities to its citizens."iv More than nice sentiments, these are even noble aspirations. But Alec Baldwin, like Jennifer Lopez, is seen as a bit flaky by both sides. Baldwin tries to connect to the powerless side. He wants to identify with and help the poor and powerless. People on the Individualistic extreme see that as phony (or worse, un-American). However, he's not necessarily acknowledged or accepted on the Enmeshed side. Rather than understanding both sides, he is at home with neither.

This applies to everyone who doesn't understand the shift. If you look at people who have tried to identify with minorities, there are some who have tried to become a minority. People on the powerless side are saying, "we don't want you to become one of us, we just want you to understand who we are. You'll never be one of us." The same is said at the other end of the model.

There's a difference between moving to the center of the model and bouncing back and forth between the extremes. I think that's what Lopez is doing. "I'm here, but I want to be there. So when I go to the Bronx, I'm Enmeshed. But when I'm in LA, I'm Individualistic." Alec Baldwin does the same kind of bounce. He grew up at the Individualistic side, but he wants to be Enmeshed, and so when he's in Latin America or on the picket line, he's Enmeshed.

The difficulty is that when people at the Enmeshed extreme see people come and try to be Enmeshed (or powerless), they basically say, "You're not one of us. You can go home any time you want. Just let us get on with our business." And it doesn't matter whether they're people of color or not. Take Jesse Jackson. Enmeshed people, even in the black community, don't look at Jackson as "one of us." They'll look at him and say that they appreciate some of the things he's done, but they don't believe Jackson can identify with them. He makes more money. He's got one kid who owns a Budweiser distributorship and another who's in Congress. They might say to him, "So you're not one of us. We appreciate the fact that you've been here, and that you understand what it is to be here, but you're no longer here." And of course, the Individualistic extreme takes a Jesse Jackson and says, "You have a lot of corporate savvy, you've made a horrendous amount of money, but you're not one of us. Because you still think Enmeshed."

For American society in terms of the model, there needs to be both a presence and a mindset. Being there, having the presence, doesn't mean you have the mindset. Wholeness is not achieved by bouncing to the other side, by becoming Individualistic or Enmeshed. Because both extremes are pathological, wholeness is found by both extremes moving to the center. Wholeness is achieved by understanding the differences between the two extremes and realizing that one side has no more value than the other. Wholeness is being at home, comfortable, in the center.

## Movies on the Model

As I hinted at in chapter one, the popularity of the recent *My Big Fat Greek Wedding* typifies the changing demographics in America. The movie was made for an outstandingly small $5 million. It started out slow, barely cracking $1 million on its wide-release opening. By September of 2002, though, it would hit its weekly gross high of $14 million, unheard of for a movie that had originally opened in April. When the total box office grosses were tallied, *My Big Fat Greek Wedding* had made almost $250 million (add the overseas gross, and the number grows by $127 million). Similar although less spectacular tales could be told about *Bend It Like Beckham* and the *Spy Kids* movies, other independent films featuring non-Caucasians in the major roles.

I believe that part of the appeal of these movies is the shifting demographics. If the Enmeshed extreme is more touchy-feely, then the so-called "chick flicks" are going to surge in popularity. Films that deal with emotion, love, and above all else, family will prove to be popular.

Does that mean that the Individualistic extreme doesn't deal with these topics? No. But the movies are significantly different. Take the recent Best-Picture Oscar winner *American Beauty*. While *My Big Fat Greek Wedding, Spy Kids*, and *Bend It Like Beckham* are celebrations of family, even in the midst of trying to break free (or saving the world), *American Beauty* tells the story of a man trying to reconnect. Kevin Spacey's Lester Birnham has it all, has achieved the American Dream. He lives in a large, suburban house surrounded by other cookie-cutter houses. After all, the American Dream means, to some extent, conformity. He has a job he hates, but he makes a lot of money at it. His wife sells real estate. But beneath the outward "beauty" of the American Dream lies a family whose members have become disconnected from each other and in many ways from themselves. It's a story of the breakdown and the ultimate betrayal of the American Dream.

Quite a bit different is the hit movie of the summer of 2003, *Finding Nemo*. If anyone's Enmeshed, it's Nemo's dad. He is a single parent (okay, fish) raising a disabled child. The message of the movie, as we have seen in the chapter on family, is that family is whomever you take in, whomever you are a part of and whomever is a part of you. While not an independent film, *Finding Nemo* has grossed to date almost $350 million domestically and $155 million overseas.

Which brings me to my point about linking entertainment and marketing. The credo for marketing is "give the people what they want." The logic is that if you give the people what they want, they will buy. If the want isn't there, create it.

The same logic applies to movies. Give the people what they want, and they will go see it. That's why, statistically, R-rated movies don't do as well as PG or PG-13 movies. If marketing and entertainment mean that we give the people what they want, and if the changing demographics mean that movie-goer demographics will change as well, I expect that we'll see a good deal more of these family-friendly movies.

## The Marketing of Entertainment

Entertainment is now what drives our country. Entertainment used to be something we did for fun, and everybody knew it was just for fun. It was like the military's R&R. You knew that reality and entertainment were two different things, and that the one made the other a little more bearable at times. Now, entertainment is everything.

Check out your local news channel. You can still get facts on the television news, but the facts are secondary. What's primary are the sets, the film clips they show, the good-looking anchor people. Further, the anchor people aren't professionals doing a job any longer but are entertainers, bantering with their co-anchor, telling jokes, taking ribbings. Everything is for entertainment purposes.

Entertainment runs everything we do. I won't spend the time here going into how this state of affairs came about.

That's been explained in other books, much more completely than I could do here.[5] But let me give a simplified explanation. The advent of television (you always knew television was evil, didn't you?) created a need to fill programs with information. It created a demand. In order to give us the information – all the information – we "need," programs began to be edited in such a way to maximize the time allotted. Therefore, we have quick visual cuts, to keep our attention on the screen, and we have shallow reporting because who has time for in-depth any more? We can watch a news story about a brutal murder and then a rape and then statistics on drunk driving and then a commercial for breath mints – all without taking a breath or blinking an internal eye. It should be amazing how non-confusing we find this, and yet this is how we've been conditioned.

Neil Postman talks in *Amusing Ourselves to Death* about the Lincoln/Douglas presidential debates and how they would go on for hours in the open air. They were well-attended debates, and the audience for them was well informed on the issues as well as on the debating candidates. Those debates couldn't happen today. We have an issue with boredom. While it's true that we will routinely watch five to six hours of television a day, that doesn't mean that we will tolerate a long presidential debate. We have been conditioned to take commercial breaks, to engage our brains in ten-minute intervals, to flip channels, to have a never-ending stream of images thrown at us. What could be more boring than a couple of talking heads? The need to be entertained has redefined the way we think.

Marketing is what sells a product. In our capitalist, Individualistic society, the questions are, how do we sell more, how do we become bigger, how do we become more successful? Remember the credo from above? "Give the people what they want. If the want isn't there, create it."

People today want entertainment; it has, after all, defined the way we think. So, to sell any product, any belief, any concept to the American public, make it entertaining. And because that's what people want, we market the most serious things that we can discuss, the things that shouldn't be marketed, and certainly shouldn't be marketed for entertainment's sake: politics, news, religion.

## The News, Politics, and Entertainment

If you want to make an issue, any issue, a part of the American mainstream, entertainment is the way you bring it in. Consider homosexuality. What would homosexuals have to do in order to become accepted by the American mainstream? They could march on Washington; they could write policy statements; they could petition; they could boycott. All these steps would be well and good, but all are fairly boring to a culture that craves entertainment. So, then, let's look at television. Twenty years ago, or even ten, there weren't a lot of homosexuals on television. There was the infamous Jodie Dallas, played by Billy Crystal, on "Soap" in the late 1970s and early '80s. But there wasn't much else, and if there was, it was scandalous (which "Soap" was during its early days, and for more than just the homosexual character). Now, every night of the week you're going to see at least one gay character, and in some cases he or she will be the main character. It began when a few television shows and movies began showing homosexuals in small roles – small but sympathetic. Once that became generally accepted, the gay characters showed up a little more prominently. Today, it's not odd at all to have a gay character or a gay talk-show host. It's because of entertainment. The gay community could not have achieved it otherwise. The issue was brought into the mainstream on the emotional side. Therefore, it caught on quickly, certainly more quickly than policy statements would have done.

An example of the emotional appeal regarding homosexuality happened at the "Rock the Vote in Boston" Democratic debate on November 4, 2003. The question was asked about gays in the military. Former General Wesley Clark was the first candidate asked. Clark said basically that gays have always served in the military, and they've done a great job. It's had nothing to do with how they serve. He said that we need to revisit the "don't ask don't tell" policy, because it hasn't worked in all areas. Others answered, and some shared statistics. Then John Kerry brought down the house with a very emotional response.

> There is a cemetery, the congressional cemetery in Washington D.C. where there is a tombstone. And the tombstone says, 'My country gave me a medal for killing a man and gave me a dishonorable discharge for loving one.' I have always fought for the right of people to be able to be treated equally in America . . . we're going to have a country where everybody has a right to be who they are, period.[6]

He got a standing ovation due to that touchy-feely, emotional soundbite.

Because the Enmeshed side is more emotional, and because the Enmeshed population is growing, this ability to speak not only in soundbites, but in emotional language as well, will become vital to winning presidential elections.

The line between politics and entertainment is blurring. In 1992, for example, then presidential candidate Bill Clinton appeared on Arsenio Hall's talk show. "In June of

1992, when all the polls showed that Bill Clinton didn't have a chance, he took his saxophone onto the Arsenio Hall show, put on dark glasses, and blew 'Heartbreak Hotel.' Greil Marcus, one of America's most imaginative and insightful critics, was the first to name this as the moment that turned Clinton's campaign around. . ."[7] Other politicians have appeared on television spots just as celebrities have appeared in politics. Arnold Schwarzenegger announced his intention of running for governor of California on "The Tonight Show" with Jay Leno. This blurring of the lines gives us the impression that "he's just one of us."

On Sep 14, 2003, Democratic presidential hopeful Howard Dean appeared on HBO's "K Street." In the story, Tommy Flannegan (played by John Slattery) accepts a job offer for James Carville to prep Dean for a presidential debate. So they prep him for a race question: Only 2 percent of the population in Vermont is African American, so what experience do you have dealing with African Americans? Carville says that that can be a damaging question, so put it off with humor. It's a heavy question, but rather than give analysis to it, say something funny. Move the listeners away from the question. Everybody laughs, and then you can come back and say something meaningful. But you have to diffuse the question first. So, Carville recommends, say that if the number of African Americans in your state determine how you get along with African Americans, if that's the standard, then Senator Lott should be Martin Luther King, Jr. Everybody laughs.

The next time Dean was at a debate, that particular question did come up, asked by an African-American reporter. And Dean gave the exact answer that he was recommended to give on "K Street." It worked. Of course, they tried to give him flak about it later, that it had been used in a fictional program, but it was too late by then.

Entertainment had done its job by deflecting the seriousness of the issue. The response had done what it was meant to do. The people can forgive dishonesty, they can forgive your stand on an issue, but they won't forgive you for not being entertaining. Entertainment excuses all.

At the "Rock the Vote in Boston" debate, after things had got a little heated over Dean's mention of the Confederate flag, a young lady in the audience (ironically named Trustman) asked, "It's not quite boxers or briefs, but I do want to ask whether it's PC or Mac?" It was a light question after dealing with heavier issues. Afterward, it was revealed by Trustman that the question was planted by CNN. The producer gave her the question! She wanted to change the question to "What part will technology play in your cabinet," but the producer told her to keep the question that she had been given.

In other words, things are getting too heavy, too serious. Let's lighten it up. Let's make it more entertaining.

I was at Barnes and Noble the other day looking at books in the politics section (I'm a political junkie). I was amazed at the number of books in that section that had words like "lies," "traitor," or "treason" in them. They are books filled with hate words, total put-downs of the other side. And yet they're all very entertaining. You can't sell a book unless it's entertaining, and taking potshots at the other side is entertaining. One of the books on the bestseller list right now is Al Franken's *Lies: And the Lying Liars Who Tell Them . . . A Fair and Balanced Look at the Right*. Franken is also the author of *Rush Limbaugh Is a Big Fat Idiot*. Entertaining titles, both of them. They should be entertaining because Franken is a comedian. (I think that Rush Limbaugh is a comedian as well, but that's another book.) It says a lot when you have Al Franken on the bestseller list, a comedian writing a bestseller about politics. That's entertainment.

The demand to be entertained and to be entertaining has shaped how we think. We take serious issues and make them entertaining. And yet, paradoxically it would seem, politicians can make outrageous statements and we take them seriously. It's not paradoxical at all if you consider that making everything entertaining lessens our ability to think critically. Consider once again the new governor in California. First, Schwarzenegger was elected without anyone really knowing what he was going to do, no policy statements (how boring are those!), but he had an image. People knew who he was. He's the Terminator. But how crazy does it get when Schwarzenegger is accused of groping several different women, gets elected anyway, and then says that he's going to hire his own private investigator to investigate himself; he then has the audacity to say that he might not share the results of that investigation with the attorney general. And nobody laughed! We took it seriously. It's ridiculous how crazy that is, but no one laughed at the press conference, no one called him on it. That's the country we live in.

Politics is such a game. We no longer want limits on the spending for a presidential campaign. If a candidate can raise $200 million, the bulk of that money is going to be spent on entertainment, on 30-second spots. The candidate will hire the best marketing gurus to put together a commercial. Elections will be (and have been) won or lost on that 30-second commercial.

The marketing of entertainment has affected how we look at the war in Iraq. We're in a war right now that's not based on reality at all. We went in with a Star Wars mentality that we could go in and end the war in three weeks. The administration accuses the news media of not telling the good parts of what's happening in Iraq, that all they're showing is the bad news. So the administration wants to spin the war. President Bush wants the media to show the positive aspects of the war, not just the negative. And yet, with all the so-called negative press, the media hasn't shown what devastation the war has caused in Iraq or talked about the body counts of the Iraqis who have been killed. We can't show those things, if we're going to keep morale high, keep interest in the war high. What would the mood of the country be if the media were showing that thousands of Iraqis, including a large number of civilians, had been killed? Some are calling the Iraq war another Vietnam, and the early body counts certainly reflect that. Medact, the British affiliate of the Nobel Peace Prize-winning International Physicians for the Prevention of Nuclear War, estimates the total civilian deaths to be between 7,000 and 10,000.[8] At what point would people say, "They're no better off than they were with Saddam"? We can't show that kind of civilian body count and still have support for the war. So the administration asks that the war be made more entertaining and less harsh.

This is the only country and the only people who can find a war entertaining. That's how far we've moved, that we can sit and watch a war on television and be entertained. That's pretty sick.

A recent movie speaks to the issue of the blurring of information and entertainment. *Shattered Glass* tells the story of Stephen Glass, former writer for *The New Republic*, and his downfall as it was discovered that he had fabricated over half of the news stories credited to him. When his editor Chuck Lane discovers the lies, he tells his staff that they have to go through every article that Glass had done to try and make things right. He says, "We let him get away with it, because it was entertaining. And that's indefensible."

Indefensible indeed.

# Reality?

I said earlier that the war in Iraq wasn't based on reality. This is the problem with entertainment. It removes us away from reality. Entertainment is about losing reality. I used to go to the movies to escape from reality because I deal too much with reality during the week. I had to have that time to veg out just a bit. I don't have to do that any longer. I can veg out all week long because life has become entertainment.

It's interesting that the more we move away from reality, the more "reality" programming we have on television. It may be a move to try to get some grounding. The further we move away from reality, the more we try to bring it back. It's a way to create entertaining reality, which takes it out of the realm of reality. But reality shows, for all the hype, aren't very real. Quantum physics teaches us that objects behave differently when they're observed. No matter how much you try to make a show appear real, it's not. Reality television would be going down the street and saying, "Let's stop at that house and see what that family is like." But that would be too boring, no entertainment to it. What's entertaining about a couple griping about going to work every morning and getting the kids off to school and not being able to afford new shoes? That's not entertainment.

Reality shows can, however, be understood in terms of the model (everything can, you know that by now). On the Individualistic extreme, we see shows like "Survivor." It's cut-throat and competitive. You get to vote people off the island (or wherever). Success means me at the top alone. The only thing that might be more Individualistic would be to have a reality show about a CEO husband and attorney wife. On the Enmeshed side, we have shows like

"Temptation Island." It's about relationships and who is with whom.

Technology is moving us even further away from reality. In Elkgrove, Illinois, the mayor and city council are trying to outlaw digital camera telephones because they're being used in locker rooms. It's an invasion of privacy. The phone companies are arguing to go ahead and outlaw them in locker rooms or workout rooms, but certainly don't outlaw them all together. Another argument was that there's a fine line between the invasion of privacy and entertainment. (Funny how we don't make those distinctions when it's celebrities whose privacy is being made into entertainment, a la "Celebrities Uncensored.") It started with video cameras, and people videotaping airplane crashes or crimes, videotaping people's private moments of grief or of intimacy. But it's entertainment! we cry. There's no such thing as privacy in the quest for entertainment.

Competition, which is on that highly Individualistic extreme, demands more and more marketing, which means more and more entertainment and less reality to what we're doing. I believe that we can take each of the other issues in this book and trace what entertainment has done to them. Consider education again. The voucher system (see chapter 4) will come down to competition. Which school is better, which one offers more? How do you market that? (Because if you don't market it, you will lose out.) We talk about obesity being a major problem for the youth in this country. But we allow Coca Cola and Taco Bell to put their food and drink in school cafeterias. That's competitive marketing, that's turning education into entertainment. It's certainly not based on the best interest of the child.

## The Church

And yet, despite all of this, the church is silent. It has not only gone along with the marketing agenda, but has been consumed by it. (More will be said about this in Chapter 9.) The primary questions in the church today are, how do we bring people in the door, and how will we raise money? Because entertainment has influenced everything we do, we sell the church the same way we sell Budweiser.

Dr. Justo Gonzalez, author and theologian, said one time that we take the "Kentucky Fried Chicken" approach to church planting. KFC doesn't open restaurants where people need chicken; they open them where they can afford chicken. And we do the same thing with the church. We no longer take the Holy Spirit to where the Holy Spirit is needed; we take the Holy Spirit to where the people are who can afford the Holy Spirit. In the Scriptures, that used to be called simony. That's what we're doing now. Who can afford it, who will buy it, and how do we market it. Church growth and church planting have become the means by which we market the Holy Spirit.

We recently disbanded Church of the Rockies, the church I had pastored for a good number of years. It was a real growing experience for me. It took me back to the Scriptures to dig into what church is about. In the midst of that, the denomination looked at mission statements created a few years ago as well as the ten-year goal that was created last year. The ten-year goal was to plant a thousand churches in ten years and become the fastest growing denomination. I looked at that and realized that we've turned God's mission upside down. The mission of every church now is to take God to a broken, hurting world, or something to that effect. The church taking God to the world. It strikes me that the Scriptures say that it is God's mission to take the church to the world. We've put ourselves in the driver's seat. So we formed a little bunker called Church of the Rockies, and that's going to be where we dig in, and from there we'll take God out to the community. That's not biblical. The Bible is about sending God's people out, not about bringing them in. It's not about making us comfortable in this one place. If we stop and think about where we can be most effective for the kingdom of God, we can be most effective by moving out of the bunker.

The response at first was "But this is our little church, we've been here for 45 years and we'll never find a place like this." However, people are now excited about going out and impacting other places. It was a fine church, but it has served its purpose.

We have such a view in this country of failure that if you close something down it's because it failed. There is a dry cleaner in Denver who has been operating his business for years, and he's always laundered my shirts. He told me not long ago that he's closing the shop. He said it had served its purpose. It put two kids through college, built a retirement nest for him and his wife, he's getting up in years, he'd like to travel, and so he bought a motor home. He said, "When I set it up, that's what I was hoping to get out of it, and it's done." If you drove by, though, and saw the cleaners with a sign in the window saying "out of business," chances are the immediate assumption would be that the guy went belly up – he failed. But, as he said, it had fulfilled its purpose, so it's done.

Church of the Rockies was set up forty-five years ago to reach the Dutch people in my community. There have been forty-five years of Dutch people going through here, and there aren't any more. Now we have Latinos. We started a Spanish congregation. Their congregation is growing, ours was not, so it seemed to me that if we looked at it honestly, we could say we've had a heck of a run for forty-five years. God planted us here to accomplish a mission, and we did it well. And now he has something else, so it's time for us to get out of the way.

That's not the kind of thinking we do in the church. That is because we see the church the same way we see everything else, as a business that needs to be marketed. Church growth and evangelism programs are all geared on that business model. Entertainment is what drives marketing today, and marketing is what drives business, and so we've allowed marketing to drive the church. Entertainment moves us away from reality, and the church is no different. People can't hurt in church. We won't allow suffering in church. The church is for those who are doing well. We say to ourselves, "We're doing a lot better than the world because we go to church." That's marketing thinking.

Marketing people hate the Scriptures that talk about "count the cost," "empty yourself," "give up everything including and especially yourself." How do you do a commercial with that? And yet people are dying for that kind of belonging, that sense of being part of something bigger than themselves, giving themselves up for something. People will give themselves up for everything else. Look at football fanatics, even during losing games. Or alcoholics who live to drink. We give ourselves up for all these other things that have become a driving force in our lives, but somehow we can't face doing that for God.

Even some of the seminary professors at both Denver Seminary and Iliff School of Theology had the reaction, "You can't close a church." Why not? It's just a building. It's not like I'm telling the people "Leave Christ." There are a lot of great programs in our community that we don't have the resources to offer. Your kids should be in a great program, so go find one. Some have asked me, "What kind of message does it give to the community to close the church?" I respond, "What kind of message does it give to the community when it's pretty dead anyway?" We took our building and gave it to the Spanish-language church, and it's growing. Some may think, "But it's ours and we're not ready to give it up." I'm saying, "It's not ours anyway and never has been."

Jesus Christ, and the church of which he is the head, is supposed to be the call to reality, but that doesn't fit our culture. The church should be the one saying that entertainment can't continue to drive politics, education, news, and religion. But that's not the case today. We've taken the anchor, the rock, the unmoving and unchangeable God and tried to make him marketable. Because marketing principles have taken over the church, we've packaged God the way we want him.

When we move so far away from reality that we have to create unreal reality, we're pretty far gone. What's amazing to me is that our kids grow up thinking this is reality. So the next generation is going to be further away from reality than we are, and it just keeps going. At some point, we have to ask where will it end?

## Questions for Reflection

Which group will be required to have an "extreme make-over"?

Can we live with somebody else's taste?

Are we running out of people to entertain?

## Summary: Entertainment and Marketing On the Model

The Individualistic extreme is typified by such movies as *American Beauty* with its desire to reconnect relationships, and such reality television shows as

"Survivor" with its competitive, everybody out for themselves, premise. Because of the drive to compete and be successful, the Individualistic extreme looks to marketing to define entertainment. Their slogan is "give the people what they want" with the hidden agenda that that is what will make more money.

The Enmeshed extreme is typified by such movies as *My Big Fat Greek Wedding* with its celebration of family, and such reality television shows as "Temptation Island" with relationships being the primary thrust. The Enmeshed extreme looks at marketing as entertainment. We want to be entertained, so with the growth of the Hispanic population, relational and familial shows will do well.

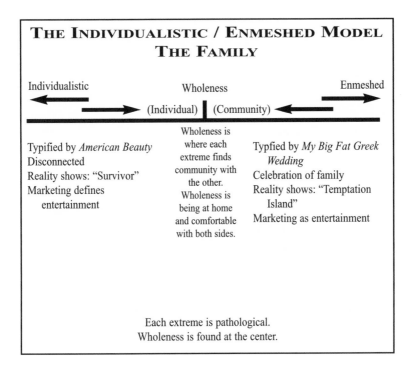

**THE INDIVIDUALISTIC / ENMESHED MODEL**
**THE FAMILY**

Individualistic       Wholeness       Enmeshed

(Individual) | (Community)

Typified by *American Beauty*
Disconnected
Reality shows: "Survivor"
Marketing defines
entertainment

Wholeness is where each extreme finds community with the other. Wholeness is being at home and comfortable with both sides.

Typfied by *My Big Fat Greek Wedding*
Celebration of family
Reality shows: "Temptation Island"
Marketing as entertainment

Each extreme is pathological.
Wholeness is found at the center.

# Notes

[1] Heather Grimshaw, "Loving Latino Lit: Hispanic Authors, Topics Hot Among Book Publishers," *The Denver Post*, Sep 28, 2003, 1EE.

[2] Michael Valdez Moses, "Back to the Future: The Nostalgic Yet Progressive Appeal of Wizards, Hobbits, and Jedi Knights," www.reason.com, July 2003.

[3] Commissioner Gloria Tristani, speech to MANA de Albuquerque, Aug 24, 2001.

[4] Leslie Van Buskirk, "The Confidence Man," *US*, May 1991.

[5] See Neil Postman's *Amusing Ourselves to Death, The Disappearance of Childhood*, and *Technopoly*.

[6] From the "Rock the Vote in Boston" transcript.

[7] From the publishers (Henry Holt & Company, Inc.) of Greil Marcus' *Double Trouble: Bill Clinton and Elvis Presley in a Land of No Alternatives*, 2000.

[8] Derrick Z. Jackson, "US Stays Blind to Iraqi Casualties," *New York Times*, Nov. 14, 2003.

# Chapter 8

## Politics: Welcome to the Party

There is perhaps no area greater to see the divide between Individualistic and Enmeshed and the grasp for power as in politics. While it may be tempting to label either side as Republican or Democrat, we can find both parties on either extreme of the model. Terms that apply more aptly to the model are conservative and liberal.

Generally, the conservative side tends to be primarily white males and white married females, while the liberal side tends to be primarily people of color and single white females. How will the changing demographics, the browning of the nation, affect politics? In many ways. Firstly, as we saw in the 2000 election, the two-party system is beginning to break down. We're hearing debates on the voting system itself, which includes debates about the workability of the Electoral College system and whether it should be thrown out or retained, as well as the continuing feasibility of the two-party system. Secondly, for the first time in election history, we're seeing an all-out effort by both parties to gain the Latino vote. Our traditional (and polarized) two-party system makes this difficult. Finally, we're seeing changes in economics and the growing disparity between the rich and the poor, and a middle class that is disappearing rapidly.

In order to understand these changes, we must start with the Electoral College and how it breaks down into the Individualistic/Enmeshed model.

# The Electoral College

As described in Article II, Section 1 of our Constitution, each state is allotted a certain number of electoral votes in electing a president. Each state is given two electors, corresponding to the number of Senators, and electors based on the number of Representatives, which varies according to population. Each state will have at least three electoral votes. Currently, there are 538 electoral votes for the 50 states and the District of Columbia (the number can change based on the results of each 10-year census). To win an election, a candidate must have 270 of the 538 electoral votes.

One aspect of the Electoral College is that it is a "winner takes all" system (with the exception of Maine and Nebraska); thus, even if the margin of popular votes is close, the electoral votes all go to the winning candidate. For example, it doesn't matter if a candidate wins the popular vote by 51% or by 91%. The candidate would receive 100% of the electoral votes. In this way it is possible for one candidate to win the popular vote and another to win the electoral vote.

This was exactly the case in the 2000 presidential election. Al Gore received a popular vote of 48.38 percent of the population, while George W. Bush received 47.87 percent. Gore received half a million more votes than Bush, so why isn't he our president? Because Gore received only 266 electoral votes compared to Bush's 271.[1]

We have become the 49 1/2 percent nation. We can no longer elect a president. That's how dysfunctional we've become. The question then is what do we do with the Electoral College? If we maintain the present two-party system and the Electoral College, then every president from here on out will be voted in by minority populations and single moms. The states that have increased the most in the electoral vote since 1990 are Florida, California, and Texas, which are also the states with the most immigration. Certain states, such as New York, Illinois, Arizona, New Mexico, and Michigan also have high populations of people of color and could figure prominently in electing a president through the Electoral College system.

As I said earlier, the people in power want to remain in power, they want to maintain the status quo. The Electoral College system, though, is not the status quo the powerful want to maintain. What they want maintained is the Individualistic ideal that we talked about in Chapter 2, the ideal of the powerful. The last election, which by all accounts was a fiasco, gave the Individualists a reason to go after eliminating the Electoral College, and I think we'll see in the next couple of years Congress trying to put through an amendment to the Constitution to that effect.

There are several alternative theories proposed if the Electoral College is eliminated. The most popular, however, is that the presidential election be decided by direct popular vote. If the Electoral College is done away with and presidents are elected simply by popular vote, then the minority populations become minorities again, with very little political power. As William C. Kimberling, Deputy Director of the FEC Office of Election Administration, notes,

> Far from diminishing minority interests by
> depressing voter participation, the Electoral

College actually enhances the status of minority groups. This is so because the votes of even small minorities in a State may make the difference between winning all of that State's electoral votes or none of that State's electoral votes. And since ethnic minority groups in the United States happen to concentrate in those States with the most electoral votes, they assume an importance to presidential candidates well out of proportion to their number. The same principle applies to other special interest groups such as labor unions, farmers, environmentalists, and so forth. . . . Changing to a direct election of the president would therefore actually damage minority interests since their votes would be overwhelmed by a national popular majority.

Not that the battle is over, by any means. The Electoral College was created in part to give extra power to the smaller states, to distribute power more evenly throughout the nation. Do away with the Electoral College and you've done away with distributed power. However, in order to eliminate the Electoral College, there would need to be an amendment to the Constitution, which would take a 2/3 approval in the House and Senate and a 3/4 majority of the states to ratify the amendment. The smaller states are not likely to vote away their power. Further, the Electoral College guarantees that campaigning will be done in a large number of states, not just the large ones. The smaller states are not likely to want to give up the attention they currently receive.

The problem with the arguments either for or against the Electoral College and our present two-party system is that they are offering short-term solutions. We as Americans have a tendency to not look to the long-term, to the future. We're more reactionary than visionary, which means that we're very good at changing things without looking at how it will affect the long-term.

Politics is supposed to be driven by the people, for the people. However, there's no serious debate going on in terms of what this country is going to be like twenty years from now. We don't have the John F. Kennedys saying, "In the next fifteen years, we're going to get to the moon." If we look at it through the Individualistic/Enmeshed model it looks like this. Both sides are asking, "What's in it for me?" not "What's in it for my people long term?" The Individualistic, powerful extreme asks, "What are we going to do next week to make sure we stay in power for another week (or four years)?" The Enmeshed, powerless extreme asks, "How am I going to make it through until next week? What bones are the powerful going to throw me?" No one is looking at "What does this mean for all of us? What is the common good?"

For example, take the war in Iraq. The Individualistic side is saying, "We're the most powerful nation, and we'll control what happens. America is mighty, and we'll show our might. We are an empire." The Enmeshed side is saying, "No, we're part of a world community. We should deal with it through the United Nations. We should all go to war, but we should do it all together." Very few have stopped to ask, what about war itself? Is war wrong? Are there ways other than war to free people? It's not a question of whether we go alone or whether we go together; it's a question of whether or not we should go at all. And that's considered a very un-American question.

## The Electoral College and Popular Culture

I stated earlier that the Electoral College was set in place in part to distribute power fairly between the states. Another major reason for its establishment was to ensure that a tyrant couldn't manipulate citizens and come to power through direct vote. At the time, there was no mass communication in place, no immediate knowledge of what a candidate might be up to. It was feared by the Framers of the Constitution that without enough information about candidates from outside their own state, people would naturally vote for someone from their own state or region. The choice of president, therefore, would always be decided by the most populous states.

Some believe that this reason for establishing the Electoral College is now moot (after all, our communication systems are light years ahead of where they were) and makes the system antiquated. However, look at what Alexander Hamilton, one of the Framers, had to say in the Federalist Papers about the Electoral College:

> It was equally desirable, that the immediate election should be made by men most capable of analyzing the qualities adapted to the station, and acting under circumstances favorable to deliberation, and to a judicious combination of all the reasons and inducements which were proper to govern their choice. A small number of persons, selected by their fellow-citizens from the general mass, will be most likely to possess the information and discernment requisite to such complicated investigations.

While Hamilton isn't coming right out and saying that the population isn't intelligent enough to make an informed decision, the underlying fear is there. I'm not convinced that this fear is unfounded. Let me give you an example.

On September 4, 2003, I was watching Keith Olbermann's countdown on *MSNBC* of the top five news stories of the day. Number 5 was Iraq; Arnold Schwarzenegger having an egg launched at him on his way to a debate was also mentioned. But the number one story for the day was Britney Spears and Madonna open-mouth kissing on the "2003 MTV Music Video Awards." They interviewed Spears and asked her what her parents thought. Her mom was okay with it, and she said, "My dad, weirdly enough, he thought it was fine, too. I mean, come on ... it's Madonna." That story beat out the events taking place in Iraq. In a nation that prides itself in its democracy, on the ideal of "we are the people and we run the government," politics is far down the list of what anyone participates in. People are unwilling to debate; they're unwilling to discuss the important issues of the day. We the people may not know what the democratic candidates think about the war in Iraq, but we do know what Britney Spears' parents think about her kissing Madonna. We have settled for entertainment over thought, appearance over substance.

Rather than an informed populace, we're a people who are governed by image. As mentioned earlier, in Colorado, we're experiencing this with the break-up of Gov. Bill and Francis Owens' marriage. People have said that the governor's marriage woes are shocking. But, as Rocky Mountain News columnist Mike Littwin noted, when the divorce rate is so high, why should anyone be shocked at a marriage falling apart? The thing is, the Owenses are normal human beings like anyone else, so they're no different from those who are struggling in their marriages. However, we've had this image of them that they built in the media in order to get elected. That image was that of family and those all-important words "family values." We allow those kinds of images, and we vote for those images. Then we're shocked when the image is different from reality.

It may be an obvious example, but of the politicians in California who campaigned to be elected governor after the recall of Governor Gray Davis, at least three were actors. Arnold Schwarzenegger, who was sworn in as governor on Nov. 17, 2003, had the greatest chance of being elected just by the image he portrays in his movies. When a country is changing as rapidly as ours is, it becomes difficult for a politician to say anything without offending a bunch of people. California is more diverse than anywhere else in the country, and no matter what someone says, it's going to offend people. The objective in the last several years has been to run elections on soundbites, on television commercials, and on very few debates (which have a good chance of offending people, and which people don't watch anyway). Schwarzenegger is the ultimate move in that direction. He was unwilling to debate, he has name recognition, and he has well-known soundbites from his movies. So he ran his spots on television, had huge rallies, and didn't answer many questions, and thus become governor of California. What we're seeing in California now is what we'll see in the future all over the country.[2]

It certainly is true that our country has the ability to be more informed than did the populace of Hamilton's day. Whether or not it has the will to be informed remains to be seen. Because the Electoral College isn't going anywhere soon, and because our country is sprinting toward the New America, gaining the Latino vote in order to secure electoral votes is imperative.

## The Schizophrenic Latino Vote

Something historic happened in the Democratic debates

in early September 2003. For the first time, the first debate of the Democratic primary season was held in front of an ethnic community. On September 4, Gov. Bill Richardson of New Mexico, an Hispanic and the chairman for the Democratic party convention this year, hosted, along with the Congressional Hispanic Caucus, the debate in Albuquerque, NM, a state with a 42 percent Latino population. "Richardson, the nation's only Hispanic governor, greeted the crowd in Spanish. He said his selection was 'a recognition that minorities, and particularly Hispanic Americans, are important and that their vote will stay very strong with the Democratic Party.'"[3]

Adam Segal, who heads the Hispanic Voter Project at Johns Hopkins University, said, "To have the first debate focus on Hispanic issues and to have it simulcast on Spanish television is a really remarkable development. ... It shows how much importance the party leadership at the very highest levels is placing on outreach."[4]

Of course, the Democrats are not the only party courting the Latino vote. From the same article:

> In 1988, [Former state Republican Party chairman Edward] Lujan chaired an RNC committee, which issued a report designed to help the GOP "build coalitions within the minority and ethnic communities."

Lujan said his committee found that the critical factor in getting more Hispanics and other minorities involved in politics was to take a door-to-door, personal approach.

"Our report was pretty simple," Lujan said recently. "People want to be wanted and they want to be asked. I'm still not sure they're being asked. ... I see a lot of talk about it, but I don't know if anybody is really door-knocking and saying to Hispanics, 'I really want you involved.'"[5]

The Latino vote isn't a sure thing for either party. Traditionally, Latinos have voted 2-to-1 Democratic, but that figure isn't carved in stone as other special interest groups tend to be. The Latino population is somewhat schizophrenic in its position; we make Democrats and Republicans both work very hard for our vote. Latinos are very conservative on issues like homosexuality and abortion. That makes them more like Republicans, right? Sometimes. They are also very liberal on spending and social issues, like taking care of the elderly and the homeless, and they see no problem with government spending for those areas.

As *US News and World Report* notes, both parties see the Latino vote as "crucial to winning the White House," but Republicans may have a bit more work to do than Democrats. Many Latinos see Republicans as anti-immigrant, due in part to the party's support in 1994 of California Proposition 187, which cut social services to illegal immigrants.

> Surveys of Hispanics also show that they tend to be more supportive of expanding government than the average voter and are more worried about the economy. "The overriding issues for Latinos are bread-and-butter issues," says U.S. Rep. Raul Grijalva, a Democrat who in 2002 rode Hispanic support to win a newly created House seat in southern Arizona. "It's going to be about employment, schools, and healthcare, and the report card is not good for President Bush."[6]

On the other hand, the Individualistic message of many in the more conservative Republican party is appealing to many Latinos.

> Latino Republicans believe they can connect
> with a growing entrepreneurial class. "The
> idea of rewarding hard work and
> independence is something Hispanics can
> relate to," says Elizabeth Gonzalez-Gann,
> the owner of Jan-Co Janitorial in Tucson . . .
> "The traditional Republican message of hard
> work and family" better matches her
> own values.[7]

So which are they, Republican or Democrat, conservative or liberal? Latinos don't fit neatly into either box and that drives both parties nuts. Take the example of President Bush's nomination of Miguel Estrada to the United States Court of Appeals for the District of Columbia Circuit. Estrada, who is a partner in a D.C. law firm and has argued fifteen cases before the Supreme Court, was nominated by Bush on May 9, 2001. Then began the acrimonious arguments of whether or not to vote him in, a process which took over two years and ended ultimately when Estrada withdrew his nomination in September 2003.

President Bush knows that it will be a major coup for the party that nominates a Latino to the Supreme Court, and he wants to be the first. Miguel Estrada looked to be the perfect candidate. He's an ultra-conservative, meaning he fits in well with the Republican party, and can swing the now-balanced Circuit Court to the right. Estrada is also young, in his early forties, which means he would sit in the Court for the next 30 or 40 years. By nominating him, Bush is appealing to the Latino vote; he is saying that he knows that Latinos are conservative and that they are ready to take their place in the leadership and law-making decisions of this country.

Democrats, as could be expected, opposed Estrada's nomination because of his conservativism, and their opposition put Estrada on hold for two years. As C. Boyden Gray, a former White House legal counsel who worked for Estrada's confirmation, said, "They did not oppose Estrada because he was Hispanic. They opposed him because he was President Bush's Hispanic."[8]

Hector Flores, the national president of The League of United Latin American Citizens (LULAC), encouraged the confirmation of the first Latino to the DC District Court. In a press release, he accused the Senate Democrats of discrimination against the Latino community and called for them to confirm Estrada. "The 41 million Hispanic Americans in the United States await your answer."[9]

However, as much as Flores might think that he speaks for all the Latinos in this country, there were many groups against Estrada's nomination, such as the National Council of La Rasa, the nation's largest Hispanic organization. The Congressional Hispanic Caucus opposed Estrada because he has not demonstrated a commitment to Hispanic causes.

And Latinos aren't the only ones unhappy with President Bush's choice. Emil Guillermo, an Asian Pacific-American, writes, "Ask yourself if we really need another right-wing Republican who might take a stand against issues impacting women, labor, equal opportunity and fairness? We need minority representation on our courts. But a brown token who votes with the white majority does not bring balance to the court."[10]

Guillermo's point is well taken. The powerless eventually become the powerful. In the Individualistic/Enmeshed model, there may be a sense of community among those on the Individualistic side, but they don't "hang out" with the powerless or disenfranchised, no matter what their ethnicity. *Rocky Mountain News* columnist Paul Campos notes this in his discussion of Estrada. He tells how the Republicans make Estrada out to be an "up-from-the-bottom immigrant" while he is in reality the son of a lawyer.

Others make him out as a Latino "uncle Tom," as he would "favor people with money and power, rather than the downtrodden." However, Campos states, "This is as absurd a mischaracterization as any indulged in by Estrada's supporters. After all, Estrada's 'people' are precisely those with money and power. That's what it means to be a member of the upper classes."[11]

Whether or not you agree with the Republicans or the Democrats regarding the nomination of Miguel Estrada, you can see clearly how each extreme, the conservative and the liberal, the Individualistic and the Enmeshed, pull toward the poles, particularly when they see their side as being threatened by the other.

Another example of the schizophrenic Latino vote was the 2003 governor recall in California. Latinos were split almost down the middle, with 46 percent supporting Gov. Gray Davis' recall and 54 percent opposing it. "'Latinos showed that they're definitely the swing voters in California. No one campaign was able to consolidate the Latino vote,' said Marcelo Gaete, senior director of programs for the national Association of Latino Elected and Appointed Officials Educational Fund. 'Latinos are up for grabs . . . To use the cliché, we are the new soccer moms.'"[12]

As these examples show, the Latino vote isn't monolithic. In fact, Latinos themselves aren't monolithic. They are divided among Mexican-Americans, Puerto Ricans, Cuban-Americans, and Central and South Americans. They haven't been as monolithic in their politics as the African Americans have been, so it's harder to determine exactly how they will vote. It's impossible to say that Latinos as a group are conservative or liberal. Those labels reflects the nature of America's two-party system, a system that is broken. As long as we're split down that way on key issues, it's going to be difficult to confirm justices for the Supreme Court or for Congress to get much accomplished.

## The Disappearing Middle Class

As I stated in the chapter on business, for a number of reasons the middle class is disappearing. This affects our two-party political system as well. Republicans work for the most powerful people in the system. It has long been considered the party for the upper class. People become more conservative when they have something to conserve, so the powerful, Individualistic extreme, which wants to conserve the status quo, is typically Republican. Democrats have traditionally worked for the second most powerful group of people, the middle class. No one really wants to work for the powerless, the poor.

In America, though, the middle class is the group that is declining the fastest. That's why the Democrats are losing their shirts and their power along with it. The people whom their message is for aren't around anymore. But the Democrats don't get that. There's still the assumption in this country (by both parties) that the people in the middle are moving to the upper class, and that the lower class people are moving to the middle (the American Dream). That's not the case, as we looked at in the business chapter. The sudden rise and fall of the dotcom industry, the off-shoring of corporate jobs, and immigration have changed the way the game is played. Only the assumptions haven't changed, and so the Democrats will still lose out.

A true third party is needed. Well, you might argue, what about Ross Perot? He tried to run on a third party and withdrew when he saw it wasn't going to work, right? Or, what about Ralph Nader? He ran on a third party in the 2000 election and received less than 3 percent of the popular vote. So why am I talking about the need for a third party? Because we haven't had a true third-party candidate. Ross Perot is about as Republican as they come, and Ralph Nader is about as Democratic as they come. Perot campaigned to the wealthy; Nader campaigned to the middle class. The numbers, though, show that maybe people should be campaigning to the lower class. I could become president with a tenth of the money Perot spent, because I would put a campaign together for the powerless group. If you could get the powerless to revolt, you'd take over the country, because the numbers are there to do it.

The last president who tried to pull the two groups – powerless and middle – together was Bill Clinton. That's why he was also called our first black president. (He was also inducted into the Arkansas Black Hall of Fame as an honorary member – the first non-black to be recognized. The honor was in recognition of his appointment of blacks to high government positions and his post-White House efforts to fight AIDS.) He had passion, and he really connected with people. People identified with him. He was born poor, was raised working-class in a single-parent household. Bush, on the other hand, has a mansion, which is nicer than Camp David. A lot of people can't identify with him.

If the Democrats want to have a say any longer in governmental policy, they must start trying to reach the powerless. I believe that Howard Dean tried. For example, early in his candidacy, Dean put together his "Sleepless Summer Tour."

> The trip is called the "Sleepless Summer Tour," but not because Dean won't get any sleep during its four days. He will. The name is a swipe at President Bush's policies and his monthlong vacation at his ranch in

Crawford, Texas. "While the president was sleeping in Texas, we are going to be out talking to people who are sleepless because they don't have health care, don't have good education and their kids are fighting in Iraq," Dean said in a telephone interview before his kickoff rally Saturday evening.[13]

Dean touched the college campuses, poverty people. The people he talked about are the powerless, those without jobs, those without health care. You can see again the breakdown in the model between the two extremes. The Enmeshed, more liberal extreme states that we need to take care of those without health care, that we should subsidize Medicare for everybody. The Individualistic extreme, on the other hand, is saying that they should be able to get the best and if the other side can't afford it, tough. And right now, the powerless are responding to his message. Give it another ten years, and those college kids will be upper class, but right now, they're middle or lower, and he tapped them. He had 280,000 contributors, and raised more than $40 million – more money than any Democrat in history in the year before the vote. He raised $14.8 million in the third quarter, more than any other Democratic presidential candidate has done in a single quarter. He did this by stating that he wants to take politics away from the status quo and put it back in the hands of the people. If Democrats can do that, they might reclaim and retain the presidency.

## Questions for Reflection

Is the system broken?

Can it work again?

How do we satisfy the continually changing special interest groups?


# Summary: Politics on the Model

People at the Individualistic extreme are conservative in their politics because they have more to conserve. They are generally white males and white married females. Because

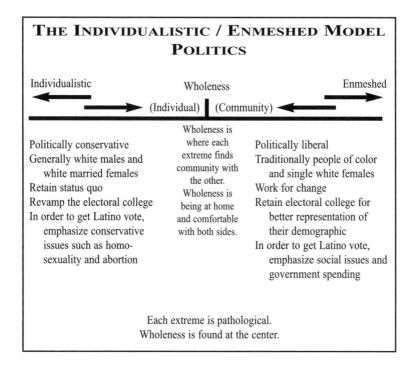

**THE INDIVIDUALISTIC / ENMESHED MODEL POLITICS**

| Individualistic | Wholeness | Enmeshed |
| --- | --- | --- |
| | (Individual) \| (Community) | |

| | Wholeness is where each extreme finds community with the other. Wholeness is being at home and comfortable with both sides. | |
| --- | --- | --- |
| Politically conservative | | Politically liberal |
| Generally white males and white married females | | Traditionally people of color and single white females |
| Retain status quo | | Work for change |
| Revamp the electoral college | | Retain electoral college for better representation of their demographic |
| In order to get Latino vote, emphasize conservative issues such as homosexuality and abortion | | In order to get Latino vote, emphasize social issues and government spending |

Each extreme is pathological.
Wholeness is found at the center.

they are the people in power, they want a system that will retain the status quo. This may mean working to jettison the electoral college. They know that the Latino vote will become more and more important as demographics change, so they emphasize the issues that Latinos feel more conservatively about, namely homosexuality and abortion.

People at the Enmeshed extreme are liberal in their politics, willing to share what they have with a community. They are generally people of color and single white females. Most likely, they will work to retain the electoral college because they are better represented there. With the importance of the Latino vote, liberals will work to ensure their vote by emphasizing social issues and government spending.

## Notes

[1] Contrary to public opinion, which has stated that this is the first time in history that the Electoral College has differed from the popular vote, there were actually three other elections when the candidate leading the popular vote did not win the office. There were also two elections where no candidate received a majority of electoral votes and were decided upon by the House of Representatives. For more history or statistics, see the Federal Election Committee's website at www.fec.gov.

[2] For an excellent discussion of how image dominates and eventually trivializes politics, see Neil Postman's *Amusing Ourselves to Death*.

[3] "No Tea, but Democrats Get the Party Started," *The Washington Post*, July 29, 2003.

[4] "Hispanic Voters Hold Key to 2004, Gov. Says," *Albuquerque Journal*, July 27, 2003.

[5] Ibid.

[6] Reed Karaim, "Latin Swing," *US News and World Report*, Sep 8, 2003, 14.

[7] Ibid.

[8] "Embattled Judicial Nominee Miguel Estrada Withdraws Name," *Associated Press*, Sept. 4, 2003.

[9] Statement given on Feb. 11, 2003.

[10] Emil Guillermo, "Miguel Estrada: Model Minority Judge?" www.AsianWeek.com, Feb 21-Feb 27, 2003.

[11] Paul Campos, "Our Dirty Little Secret," *Rocky Mountain News*, Sep. 9, 2003, 31A.

[12] Beth Fouhy, "Arnold Introduces Team," *Rocky Mountain News*, Oct. 10, 2003.

[13] Nedra Pickler, *Associated Press*, August 24, 2003.

# Chapter 9

## The Church in America: Whose Idea of an Answer?

A s anyone who has ever encountered a Christian knows, most Christians, myself included, think that they have the answers to the world's ills. While some may hold that belief in an arrogant, judgmental manner, the belief actually stems from Jesus who said, "I am the way, the truth, and the life." While we may agree that not every problem the world faces is found in the pages of the Bible, we generally feel that a belief in Jesus Christ will make things better.

If that is the case, then we would expect the church to have the answers to the issues we've examined in this book. If anyone has the answer to overcoming the extremes and coming to the center, it should be the church. So what does the church say?

Unfortunately, we find the same extremes in the church. If we look at politics, we find liberal and conservative Christians, those who believe that the gospel's primary purpose is social justice and those who believe that it is evangelism. In education, we again find Christians on both sides of the model.

The church is the body of people who should be bringing us the message of wholeness. And yet the church is full of people who are just as shrill and just as extreme about politics, education, the family, business, and the rest as anyone else. The reason? The church today has lost sight of wholeness. The church today has broken down into the same pathological extremes.

## The Pathology of the Church

Since the events of September 11, 2001, we have become a nation where the greatest sin is a lack of patriotism. For some, even questioning President Bush's decisions on sending troops to war with Iraq is tantamount to treason. We hear often, particularly from liberals, that war is wrong. We hear often, particularly from conservatives, that maybe free speech in the form of criticism of the government should be denied to liberals. And we hear many sermons on what it means to live in a Christian nation, or at least one that was founded on Christian principles.

From the conservative side, we might hear about Patrick Henry who said, "It cannot be emphasized too strongly or too often that this great nation was founded, not by religionists, but by Christians, not on religions, but on the gospel of Jesus Christ." Or perhaps of John Quincy Adams who said, "The highest glory of the American Revolution was this: that it connected, in one indissoluble bond, the principles of civil government with the principles of Christianity." What about the father of our country, George Washington, who said, "It is impossible to rightly govern the world without God and the Bible."[1]

Many Christians are fighting to keep these principles alive, to return God to public places, including public schools. We hear regularly about the battles over the Pledge of Allegiance's "under God" phrasing. We battle about the constitutionality of prayer and Bible reading in schools. We fight to keep The Ten Commandments on public display. We fight for nativity scenes in front of government buildings at Christmas.

A sermon out of a large church in California noted that while America was founded as a Christian nation, we're running from God now. We need a return to a "godly America." The benefits, the pastor said, are that a godly nation is exalted, strengthened, and blessed by God. His definition of "blessed" is to cause to prosper, to be made happy. According then to this kind of definition, Africa, which has the most Christians of any continent, and yet is also one of the poorest, isn't blessed.

This particular pastor didn't state in this sermon that it is America's ungodliness that caused the events of September 11; however, it is clear that he believes that our nation will be protected from further harm if we "stand for righteousness." Others, such as Jerry Falwell, did state that the bombing of the Twin Towers in New York could be God's just punishment upon us. On Pat Robertson's "700 Club" television show, he stated,

> The ACLU has got to take a lot of blame for this. . . . the abortionists have got to bear some burden for this because God will not be mocked and when we destroy 40 millions little innocent babies, we make God mad . . . . I really believe that the pagans and the abortionists and the feminists and the gays and the lesbians who are actively trying to make that an alternative lifestyle, the ACLU, People for the American Way, all of them who try to secularize America . . . I point the

thing in their face and say you helped this happen.[2]

While Reverend Falwell later apologized, and said that blame lay with the terrorists, he reiterated that certain groups have worked for the secularization of America, removing it from its spiritual foundation.

Much heat has been generated over these arguments. I believe, however, that trying to return America to its Christian roots, to make America Christian once more (assuming that it truly was), is simply rearranging the deck chairs on the Titanic. It is focusing on peripheral issues while the underlying structure is the thing that's rotting. As Samuel Chand says,

> Instead of living in the future, *many pastors are trying to recapture the church of past generations*. We do this by our architecture, our styles of worship, our times of worship, and even the sermons and Sunday school lessons. . . . That's why our church highway is strewn with wrecks. We prefer to drive watching the rearview mirror rather than gazing through the windshield and facing the future.[3]

We call America a Christian nation, or insist that it was built on Christian principles, but is it biblical? Can one be a good American and a good Christian at the same time? I say no.

I can hear the protests now. I'm not suggesting that as Christians we shouldn't sing The Star Spangled Banner or say "The Pledge of Allegiance." I'm not suggesting that we become like the Jehovah's Witnesses, who believe that loyalty to country is disloyalty to religious belief. I'm not suggesting that we shouldn't vote or be part of the political process, or that we shouldn't either support or protest American involvement in Iraq.

Before we talk about the larger church in America, though, let's talk about local churches, the ones in your neighborhood, the ones you attend every Sunday. In his book The Bride: Renewing Our Passion for the Church, Chuck Swindoll breaks down our experience of church into four sections: Worship, Instruction, Fellowship, Evangelism (WIFE). It's a helpful division that I'll use here.

## WIFE: Worship

Generally, when we talk about worship in the local church, we think of the music and everything else that happens other than the sermon. (Theologically, worship involves the entire service and indeed the whole of life – but that's another book). Think for a moment about the "worship wars" going on in many churches. Most of the time, it's over music – and churches have split over it.

At the Enmeshed extreme is tradition. We might hear the phrase, "This is the way it's always been done." These are the people who frown on guitars and drums in church, and let's not even talk about drama. If a piano (or a pipe organ) was good enough for their fathers and their fathers before them, then it's good enough for them. They bemoan the loss of the great hymns that had so much theology in them.

At the Individualistic extreme are the newer forms of worship. "Contemporary worship music" started primarily as an outreach tool to get people in the door. The thinking was that if the church continued to play stodgy music from hundreds of years ago, no one would come. They rejected that kind of worship when they rejected other things from their childhoods. What the church needed in order to draw in others was to play the music that people heard everyday on their radios. And, yes, it worked. People came in, many times in droves. And they stayed. Now they are demanding that church cater to them in every way possible and it had better be entertaining. Who can blame them, when the church pandered to their Individualistic wants to get them there in the first place?

Many people in the Individualistic extreme treat worship like a business. The introductory music and prayers, in older times known as "the call to worship," are only the small talk before the real event: the sermon. Therefore, if people need to get to church late, they're not really missing anything important.

Today, worshipers are consumers and church is the product. If we want someone to attend our church (how competitive is that!), it behooves us to offer a better product. "Convenience and customization will determine attendance at church and worship events. Consumerism dominates attendance, where shoppers for the faith are looking at what a particular church has to offer them in child care, timing of services, proximity to home, easy parking, musical style, and preaching that suits them."[4]

In both of these extremes, the emphasis is on "me" and what "I" get out of worship, when worship should always be first and foremost about God.

## WIFE: Instruction

Instruction in many ways follows the way secular education has gone. As I talk about it, instruction refers to the sermon and to Sunday school. The Enmeshed extreme prefers their sermons to be in story-form. They relate to Jesus' parables. When the pastor tells stories from his or her own life, it helps the Enmeshed to feel connected. For the Enmeshed, relationship is primary, and so with personal stories, these people can feel that they know the pastor.

The sermons on the Individualistic extreme look and sound like school. The local church may even print an outline of the sermon in the bulletin so the congregation can take notes. The Individualistic person wants his or her mind to be challenged.

Sunday school emphasizes "school." Generally, it's high teaching and low relationship. Bible studies are competitive. Homework may be assigned. The professor, I mean the leader, assigns chapters of the Bible for weekly study during people's misnamed "devotionals." Then the class meets to study the passage and ask and answer questions. People who don't do well in school or in this kind of competitive learning environment won't go back to this kind of class. They don't have the answers and so feel stupid. They also feel disconnected, because relationships are minimized.

What we need to ask, though, is what is Bible study for? It should be transformational (as should worship, fellowship, and evangelism). We're not in the business of winning competitions; we're in the business of changing lives. Instruction for any other purpose is simply vanity.

If a Sunday school class tries to be relational, it very often ends up being competitively relational. When I was in seminary, a large local church hired me to do an evaluation of their church practices. This church had a very successful small group. It had grown so fast and so large that it split off into other groups, and in this way kept growing as they "discipled" other people. The group? Gourmet cooking. They met in each other's homes, and I visited one week. There was no prayer, no discussion of family matters, no talk about the Bible; in short, nothing was transformational. They talked about the foods they had eaten and the travels they had been on – and that was where the competition came in as each couple tried to one-up the others on their travel stories. There was more drinking than I had seen even in my accountant days. They didn't even pray over the meal. This wasn't discipling; it was a recipe exchange. This wasn't a discipleship group; it was a social club.

## WI**F**E: Fellowship

Fellowship breaks down into the two extremes as well. On the Individualistic side, fellowship is compartmentalized with very little sense of real community. It emphasizes homogenous units, where the most successful classes fall into the sin of "differentism." There are classes for young marrieds, college singles, older singles, divorced, parents of toddlers, parents of teens, and so on. Many times the homogenous unit is based on geography – what's your zip code becomes the first question asked.

The Enmeshed side can feel very exclusive to those who aren't in the "club." It's the family where everyone else is the outsider. In Colorado, there's a great deal of pride in being a native. A friend's husband tells her that he's been in Colorado for 35 years – most of his life – so he's "practically a native." She disagrees. Unless you were born here, you're not a native. That's the attitude that many people encounter when they try to join a new church. It's likely one reason that Enmeshed churches as a rule stay small; breaking into the club is not easy.

Fellowship is difficult on the one extreme if you weren't a part of it from the beginning, or it's being shuffled into a small group based on some pigeon-holed categories.

## WI**F**E: Evangelism

The way the two extremes view Christ impacts their view of evangelism. Both of these views of Christ can be found in the Scriptures. The dichotomy is between the

Victorious Christ on one hand and the Suffering Christ on the other.

The Enmeshed extreme is powerless. They identify with Christ who had no place to lay his head and who took our sins onto himself. "He suffered under Pontius Pilate, was crucified, dead, and buried." He is the Man of Sorrows. Even the Incarnation itself is a matter of suffering, for he, the God of Heaven, took on earthly form. He can intercede on our behalf, because he himself suffered.

The Individualistic extreme focuses more on Christ's "success." "He ascended into heaven, and is seated at the right hand of the Father." He is now in a place of power. He has conquered death. The darkness of the crucifixion always gives way to the glory and joy of Easter morning.

Evangelism for the Enmeshed side begins and ends with family. The patriarch or matriarch of the family is responsible for leading the others in the family. They don't come to an "altar call" with an individual decision; they come as a family.

For the Individualistic side, evangelism is bringing them the American Dream. "All we have to do," they may say, "is reach the Enmeshed people for Christ, and they will come and be like us." Evangelism will lead to fine, productive members of society, who are hard working and enjoy competition – all the Individualistic attributes. The way the secular school system used the melting pot (assimilation) to make good citizens, the church uses evangelism. And most of the time, they don't even recognize it.

For example, in the summer of 2003 HIS Ministries partnered with InterVarsity Denver Urban Project, which brought together students studying for the ministry and urban youth. At a roundtable discussion, I overheard a group of students talking about their experiences and the realization that Vacation Bible School has changed. One example they gave was "sin bracelets," which use different colored beads to represent parts of the gospel presentation. One student thought that maybe it was offensive to urban youth (many of them minorities) to have sin represented by a brown or black bead. It was also noted how different the cultures are. One student asked, "If someone in that cultural group accepts Christ, don't they have to accept less of their culture?" Wow, it's a great question and a great observation. But what she didn't realize was that she has her own culture that needs to be less accepted as well. Too often, we in white evangelical (Individualistic) America have assumed that our culture is God-ordained and that everyone else needs to change to be like us.

We've always had an easier time evangelizing the poor and powerless. Ministry to the powerless is less intimidating. The more powerless they are, the more we can throw material possessions at them. Set up a food pantry or a soup line, and preach to them before you feed them. Donate clothes and toys at Christmas. Then put a videotape together and send it to megachurches so hopefully they'll send money so that we can keep feeding the poor. And we'll feel good about ourselves because we're "helping." But once those people become more powerful and get their own food, they won't come back to church. Evangelizing the powerless is easy, but evangelizing the powerful is difficult.

Because of the way we do evangelism, when the people we have "helped" get to a place of power, they feel they no longer need God. We've told them that in order to be saved they need to become like us. Well, now they're like us. They haven't seen the inside of a church in years. They no longer need God – that's how powerful and self-sufficient one can get in America.

# The Pathology of the Church in America

We've been talking about the local church, what you might experience when you visit the church in your neighborhood. But the pathology in these churches is simply a microcosm of the larger pathology of the church.

When we talk about America, we're talking about more than the history or the people who make it up. We're talking about an ideological viewpoint, the Individualistic extreme. Gary Wederspahn notes,

> It is possible to identify a set of centripetal (opposite of centrifugal) values that tend to hold us together and identify us as a nation. These are the official values enshrined in our major political documents and the unofficial ones that characterize the "great American dream" and shape our way of life. They are promoted by the media and our public figures and are often held as ideals rather than experienced as practical realities. Yet they do have impact on our self-concepts, influence our behavior and determine how we are viewed by the rest of the world.[5]

The things that I said in earlier chapters about the American Dream apply to the church as well, and when Wederspahn talks about the American Dream being promoted by media and public figures, I don't think we can exclude church leaders as American Dream promoters. The American Dream means bigger is better, and success is measured by more money and bigger product. It means never asking for help, in other words, pulling yourself up by your bootstraps. It means competition and educational achievement.

# The Church and the American Dream

## Bigger Is Better

Perhaps the clearest indication of the church's pathological entanglement with the American Dream is the emphasis on church growth and the Church Growth Movement. Donald McGavran, born to missionary parents in India, is credited with the beginning of the Church Growth Movement (CGM). Bothered by the poor growth of churches there, he began to study in order to rectify the problem. With a true heart of evangelism, McGavran believed that churches must embrace everything that make disciples and throw out everything that does not. "He also believed effective evangelism is something which produces results that can be counted numerically and it is much more likely to take place if the person doing the evangelizing belongs to the same culture, class, tribe, or family as the person he is trying to evangelize."[6] McGavran eventually became the founding dean of the Fuller School of World Mission at Fuller Theological Seminary in Pasadena, California.

McGavran's teachings influenced such church growth leaders as Ralph Winter, Win Arn, and John Wimber, but most noticeably C. Peter Wagner who expanded the program at Fuller and teaches the Doctor of Ministry program in church growth there. Even in the early stages, though, the movement was not without detractors, due to the movement's emphasis on homogenous units, its lack of social concern, and its burgeoning interest in healing ministries and "signs and wonders." What I want to focus on, however, is the Church Growth Movement's belief that evangelism can be measured numerically.

The CGM uses demography and market research to determine how to grow. Now, of course demography "works," if pragmatism is the means of determining success. People are uncomfortable being with people who are different. We feel comfortable with people who look like us and who are in the same economic sphere. Differentism, like racism, is a problem that we in the church must deal with, but the CGM uses differentism to get bigger numbers. Market research is used hand in hand with demography to find out what this particular demographic group likes. Is it a younger demographic? Then get a band in there. Older? Get a pipe organ. Suburban? Get attendants for the parking lot.

Furthermore, since the people CGM is trying to reach are in the business world and are used to a certain standard of performance, the church needs to make sure that everything is at a high level of quality. Baby boomers, the largest segment of the population, want informal services, informal dress, short sermons, little or no theology but plenty of practicality. And above all, everything needs to be entertaining. If you can make a church service look like a television program, then you'll draw people in; you'll have bigger numbers, which translates into success. However, it must look like whatever else is in the particular community the church wants to reach. That's the homogenous unit principle. People will come to the church that looks the most like them. This is called, at times, the "user-friendly" church.

Am I suggesting that the church not use marketing principles? No. I am, however, suggesting that we take a long look at the motivations behind using those principles. How sincere are we in reaching people for Christ? Or do we just want to look successful because we have a big, impressive building? Do we celebrate the amount given because of the way God can use it? Or do we see it as a sign of our success? Do we strive for excellence because the Lord has commanded us to give him our very best? Or do we strive for excellence because that's how it's done in the professional world? Finally, I'm concerned that the emphasis on marketing, on making church services user-friendly, on creating homogenous units makes Jesus a product. Oh yes, we're convinced that the unchurched need this product, but we treat Jesus as a product to be marketed, nonetheless. The Individualistic extreme is trying to sell the product of "Jesus and the good life."

The Church Growth Movement has many things to commend it. Some of its suggestions, such as the possibility of updating traditional worship services, are good and need to be thought through. There are some danger signs, however, that the church cannot ignore. The Individualistic extreme drives this idea of church growth and, therefore, is at times pathological.

For example, how relevant is too relevant? It is one thing to update the hymnal or to change worship times. It is another thing entirely to not preach certain portions of the Bible because they might be offensive (wouldn't want too many people leaving – that creates negative growth). The pastor can preach against homosexuality, because there probably aren't any homosexuals in the congregation anyway, and the congregation is comfortable with denouncing gays and lesbians (mainly because with homogenous units, they probably don't know any). But what about sermons on adultery? What about Christians using pornography? What about living together before marriage? That might be hitting a little too close to home. If people are squirming, maybe it's time to back off and get back to the sins they're more comfortable hearing about, the ones that don't personally impact them.

The problem with a "user-friendly" church is that sometimes, maybe even the majority of the time, the gospel isn't user-friendly. Jesus was called a scandal. Michael Card's song "Scandalon" sums it up well.

> He will be the truth that will offend them one and all
> A stone that makes men stumble
> And a rock that makes them fall
> Many will be broken so that He can make them whole
> And many will be crushed and lose their own soul.

Doesn't sound user-friendly, does it? As Kirk Wellum says, "While we must be sensitive to the needs of people around us, we must preach Christ and Him crucified, and be prepared to endure the trouble that will come our way. How we apply the Bible will vary depending on the situation we are addressing, but the essential message must not change no matter how much it rubs people the wrong way, because whether they know it or not, it is exactly what they need to hear."[7]

If we make the gospel look little different than an entertaining television program, how will it be able to impact their lives? For a world that is broken and hurting, telling people to watch an episode of "Touched by an Angel" is like putting a bandage on a knife wound. It won't stop the bleeding and it certainly won't aid the healing.

Maybe it's time we paraphrase Miriam in the Old Testament, "Some trust in marketing, some in technique. But we remember the name of our God." Success cannot be defined in terms of numbers or of dollars. For the church, success cannot be equated with the Individualistic extreme.

## Never Ask for Help

Self-reliance is a strong value of the American Dream. It's that rugged individualism again. So many pastors burn out because they can't ask for help. They can't share their struggles. What? Pastors have struggles? You bet. In a local suburban congregation, one of the ministers admitted to having an affair. About a year before, his wife had tried to talk in the women's Bible study about her marital problems, but she was shut down. No one wanted to talk about it; no one wanted to admit that pastors have problems. As the Hope Rasalam Foundation notes, "Ministers are almost alone in their struggles. There are no built-in escape valves in their profession. Most pastors cannot share their frustrations with members of the church, other pastors, their parents, or even their wives. People expect them to be pillars of strength, and if they appear to be anything less, they create insecurity in the minds of their people."[8]

You can see this attitude reflected in the bulletins of many churches. One church offered a number of groups that met on Wednesday nights. There were groups for Adult Children of Alcoholics, Parents in Pain (which dealt with parents whose kids were on drugs), families of gay and lesbians. Where are the groups for the alcoholics, the drug addicts, the homosexuals? We can ask for help when it's dealing with someone else's sin. But we can't admit our own. Why? Because it means that somehow we have failed.

One of the reasons I, through HIS Ministries, started Casa de Paz was to help pastors and their staffs deal with issues in order to prevent burn out. Our mission is to advance God's Kingdom through prayer, hospitality, and spiritual development. In my travels, I've found a tremendous hunger for prayer and spiritual direction on the part of pastors and church leaders. Most times, these church leaders cannot afford a week or two-week retreat, but they could benefit from a two-hour, half-day, or full-day prayer retreat. This helps them admit their own need of healing. Again quoting Michael Card's song, "Many will be broken so that He can make them whole." We have to learn how to ask for help if we ever want to be whole.

## Competition and Educational Achievement

Many times it feels as though the church is "circling the wagons." We feel that we're under attack and so we must form the circle in order to protect ourselves. A Catholic friend of mine has noted that when you begin your religion as a protest against something (Protest-ants), you feel more comfortable and more essential when you're against something. That describes evangelicals. We're always more comfortable when we're besieged, and so we circle the wagons.

One of the ways we protect ourselves is through the Individualistic ideal of educational achievement. Requirements for being a pastor vary widely from denomination to denomination. Some require only a bachelor's degree and a statement that one feels "called" to the ministry in order to be ordained. For some of the largest churches in America, though, ordination requires at least a post-graduate theological seminary degree. However, if a pastor wants more speaking engagements and writing opportunities, it is imperative to earn an even higher degree, either a Ph.D. degree or a Doctor of Ministry degree.

So, we have a great deal of Spanish-speaking and Korean-speaking churches that are just booming – far faster than many other evangelical churches. But we get around that by noting that "those people" aren't ordained; they haven't been to seminary and so who knows what theology they're preaching. Further, they can't be ordained unless they go to our seminaries. In that way, we can be sure that they become like us.

One problem with this, as I noted earlier in the education chapter, is that seminary doesn't really teach practical things such as how to run a church. What it does best is train future seminary professors. It is a self-perpetuating institution, geared toward the replication of others who are "just like us."

## That's Un-American!

The church has bought into the American Dream. Being a good Christian is not necessarily being a good American, and at times the church today would rather be good Americans than good Christians. We get angry if someone says that we're un-American, and what I'm suggesting sounds un-American. It is. But it's biblical. However, we'd rather continue to pursue the American Dream than pursue Christ's demands. We have such questions now as "What Would Jesus Drive?" Some say that he would drive an SUV or a minivan. After all, he would fit in with the culture, and wouldn't he want his children to be safe (as well as be comfortable with the DVD player in the backseat)? Others say that he would drive one of the new hybrid automobiles, or at least a very fuel-efficient car in order to take care of the environment. The very question was initiated by "The Evangelical Environmental Network and Creation Care Magazine because transportation is a moral issue."[9] While I'm not trying to make light of this issue, and certainly we are called upon to be stewards of the whole of creation, a few miles more per gallon of gas does not address the fact that we are still not concerned with the widows and orphans, the poor and the hungry.

We continue to have the Republican church and the Democratic church, conservative and liberal. We have Pat Robertson's Christian Coalition on one side. On the other, we have the newly formed Clergy Leadership Network to advocate on the side of liberals in this country. Like the Christian Coalition, they will not endorse candidates because of their non-profit status, but they will speak to the Democratic side of issues. Whether you agree with the Christian Coalition or the Clergy Leadership Network, this just stands as more evidence that the church cannot draw us to the center of the model, because the church has no more wholeness than anyone else. We're becoming special interest groups on both extremes.

And in the meantime, we still have the great divide between Individualistic and Enmeshed, between Powerful and Powerless.

We as Christians lay out the answers to the serious problems that face our country. However, we're impotent. We can't speak to the problems – even if we know the answer – because the church has broken down. We know the answer, but sadly enough it remains theory. We don't live it.

Two thousand years of tradition isn't working. People aren't in church. Christians aren't in church. When they go, it's the same old thing. It's true that we could put that fact out of our minds by saying, "The real Christians are in church," but obfuscating doesn't really solve the problem, does it? Maybe once we start focusing on the real problems, church worship will look different. Maybe it will happen once a month. Maybe it will happen on Tuesday nights because there's nothing else going on then.

When we learn to be of like mind with Christ, when we give up ourselves, we will become a transformational people.

## *Questions for Reflection*

Can you be a good Christian and a good American?
Is the church just another special interest group?
What can we do with the Republican national church and the Democratic national church?

# Summary: Church on the Model

According to the Individualistic extreme, the church's primary purpose is evangelism. The physical body is fleeting, what matters is the soul. Church services have become increasingly evangelistic as churches market

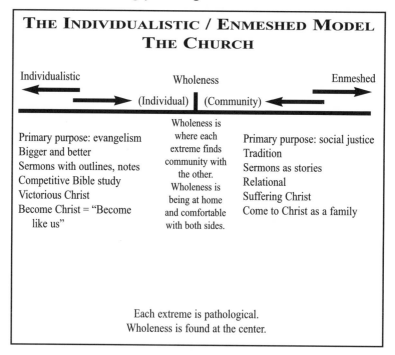

THE INDIVIDUALISTIC / ENMESHED MODEL
THE CHURCH

Individualistic          Wholeness                          Enmeshed

(Individual) | (Community)

| Primary purpose: evangelism | Wholeness is where each extreme finds community with the other. | Primary purpose: social justice |
|---|---|---|
| Bigger and better | | Tradition |
| Sermons with outlines, notes | | Sermons as stories |
| Competitive Bible study | Wholeness is being at home and comfortable with both sides. | Relational |
| Victorious Christ | | Suffering Christ |
| Become Christ = "Become like us" | | Come to Christ as a family |

Each extreme is pathological.
Wholeness is found at the center.

themselves to become bigger and better. Music resembles what the surrounding neighbors listen to in order to make them comfortable when they come in the door. Sermons are highly instructive lectures, often coming with outlines. Sunday school classes are competitive in Bible reading and often have homework in the form of Bible reading. Christ is viewed as "victorious" and, therefore, we his people will also be victorious not only over sin but over material discomforts as well. Evangelism, then, stresses for others to become like us so that they can experience victory and prosperity as well.

According to the Enmeshed extreme, the church's primary purpose is social justice. People won't listen to the message when they're starving, so feed them first. Worship forms are more traditional and thus congregations are getting older and are dying out. Enmeshed people like their sermons as stories because they tend to be more relational, which is also what their Sunday school classes are. Christ is viewed as "suffering" and, therefore, we have someone who can identify with us in our suffering and poverty. Evangelism is not a conquest but is viewed as a family matter.

## Notes

[1] It should be noted that there is a great deal of debate on whether these people actually said these words or not. For example, while George Washington may have been a man of faith, the origin of this particular saying cannot be found. Many Christians, though, continue to put this forth as evidence of a Christian heritage.

[2] From the transcript.

[3] Samuel Chand, "Futuring: No Longer Gazing in the Rearview Mirror," *Rev.,* May/June 2003, 68.

[4] Ibid., 71. Emphasis mine.

[5] Gary Wederspahn, "U.S. Cultural Baggage," 1.

[6] Kirk Wellum, "An Evaluation of the Church Growth Movement," presented to Sovereign Grace Community Church, Sarnia, Ontario.

[7] Ibid.

[8] http://www.rasalam.com/www.prayer-ministry.com/pastorburnout.html.

[9] www.creationcare.org.

# Chapter 10

## ¿Y Que Honda?

Andrea, the daughter of a friend of mine, recently spent some time in Mexico. She had a great time, and when she came back, I noticed she had picked up a lot of informal sayings or slang in Spanish. She called me on the phone, and her first words were "¿Y que honda, Pastor?" More than just the literal (and rather formal) translation of "and what's up?" this phrase more closely resembles the old Budweiser beer commercials "Whazzup?" It represents an interest in all that's gone before with a view toward what's coming. So, what's up with all of this? What's the answer?

We have been talking in the previous chapters about the two sides to everything, Individualistic and Enmeshed. Both sides are extreme. With every issue we've talked about, the separation between the two is getting wider. As a nation, we're pulling closer to the extremes rather than moving toward the center. Wholeness, though, is found in the center, and it looks a lot different than what we have now. Wholeness is where the extremes meet. Wholeness is being your own person and also having a sense of belonging. Wholeness is being an individual working for, in, and with a community.

We can see this blending in the best of the medical research profession. With the exception of movie stereotypes of the "mad scientist," researchers are a group of people, individuals with their own interests and drives, who work for the betterment of their community. True, some may also work for the personal goals, the accolades of being published in the most prestigious medical journals, or for the excitement of having a disease named after themselves. But it is work within and for the medical community and the larger community of humanity.

Or consider a sports team. We tend to get disgusted with a player who puts his own statistics and career before the team. Most players, the really good ones, feel that no matter what their personal statistics say, if they don't help the team to win, the statistics don't mean squat. What is important is what goes in the win/loss column. That's an individual with a sense of belonging and working with other individuals in the betterment of a community.

We haven't, though, really said, "Here's how to resolve the problem. Here is the center. Here is how to become whole." So, how do we draw these extremes together?

## Be of Like Mind

I'm a pastor and am prone to quote scripture at the drop of a hat. It's a hazard of the job, I suppose. But I purposely have not said much about God in this book until this time. One reason is that there are more people than just Christians reading this book, and I actually wanted them to get this far. Sometimes we Christians are so anxious to present the gospel that we forget Christ's words to be meek. In our hurry to evangelize the world, we knock people over with a sledgehammer instead of wooing them as God does.

Another reason, perhaps a greater one, is that many Christians believe that the answer to any question can be found in Jesus Christ. I believe that too, but maybe in a little different way. The truth is, Jesus Christ isn't found at the Individualistic extreme with the conservatives demanding a return to a seemingly more moral age. Nor is he found at the Enmeshed extreme with the liberals demanding social justice. Jesus Christ is himself the center. And it is only at the foot of the cross that we find wholeness.

I'd like to take Philippians 2:3-11 as the supreme example of wholeness, of coming together at the center. (For those reading this who don't consider themselves Christians, I believe these words still contain insight into the human condition. We may have different opinions of who Jesus was, but the spirit of this passage applies whether we consider Jesus to be God incarnate or simply a great moral teacher.)

> Do nothing out of selfish ambition or vain conceit, but in humility consider others better than yourselves. Each of you should look not only to your own interests, but also to the interests of others.
> Your attitude should be the same as that of Christ Jesus:
> Who, being in very nature God,
> did not consider equality with God something to be grasped,
> but made himself nothing,
> taking the very nature of a servant,
> being made in human likeness.
> And being found in appearance as a man,
> he humbled himself
> and became obedient to death—
> even death on a cross!
> Therefore God exalted him to the highest place
> and gave him the name that is above

every name,

    that at the name of Jesus every knee should bow,

        in heaven and on earth and under the earth,

    and every tongue confess that Jesus Christ is Lord,

        to the glory of God the Father. (NIV)

The center, being whole, is found in giving up of self. "Consider others better than yourselves." Individualistic extreme, can you look at the Enmeshed extreme and consider them better than yourself? Enmeshed extreme, can you look at the Individualistic extreme and consider them better? Can you at least look at the other side and admit that they make a good point? Can you by renouncing differentism come to a place of feeling comfortable, at home, with both sides?

Sometimes, we are so fearful of losing our grasp on what we consider to be important. And yet, if we have the truth – whatever we might mean by that – the truth isn't threatened by looking at the other side, by considering other options. What happens instead is understanding and a move toward wholeness.

Jesus Christ lived that understanding and that wholeness. This scripture says that even though he was equal with God, he didn't consider it something to grasp, to hold onto. Why? Because he knew it was there. It would be like me trying to hold onto my position in my family. What would be the point? It's not going to change. I will always be the sixth of ten children of my mother and my father. I don't need to grasp onto that; I don't need to make arguments for that. So, because Jesus knew himself that well, because he knew that equality with God wasn't going to change or be something to lose, he could make choices.

His choice? To give up himself. "He made himself nothing [literally, he emptied himself], taking the very nature of a servant."

What does it mean to be a servant? Do we even know any more? The servants are the ones who clean our houses, including the toilets. They prepare and serve our food. They take care of our children and our elderly. What did it mean for Jesus to become a servant? It meant that he sought first the good of his Father's kingdom, even to the point of death. He washed the disciples' feet, something that scandalized the religious leaders in his day. Rather than say, "I am the God of the universe!" he put on a towel and washed their feet. How many CEOs would have that attitude toward the mailroom clerks? And yet we are commanded in this scripture verse, "Your attitude should be the same as Christ Jesus." Be of like mind. In all the popular talk of "what would Jesus do?" we've lost the fact that the first thing Jesus would do would be to give up himself and serve others.

Many times our evangelistic attitude is "in order to achieve salvation, become like us." We believe that we are the normal ones. We have allowed the privileges of the powerful (sometimes called "white privilege") to blind us. The Apostle Paul, however, divested himself of privilege, at one point saying, "Neither Jew nor Gentile, neither male nor female," and at another point stating, "I have become all things to all people."

Manual Ortiz addressed this issue when he wrote about the problems of urban cities.

> Despite all our advances in civil rights, North Americans live in a profoundly segregated society. We have chosen to live with segregation in our schools, our neighborhoods, and our businesses. . . .

> Segregation is illegal – yet it continues with minimal response from evangelicals. If anything, we have exacerbated the problem by following the agenda of segregation and not speaking and living against it. We have chosen to keep ourselves separate rather than practice incarnational ministry by living, working, praying, and suffering with people in the city. We have learned how to do ministry from a distance. This is far from the biblical model of our Lord, who came to be with us and emptied himself.[1]

The church, in other words, must also divest itself of privilege. In our religious zeal, we have often sought victory in our battles against homosexuality, abortion, and women's liberation. The battles are real and the casualties have been many. However, when Martin Luther King, Jr. fought his battles, he used non-violence. He knew that violence would only harden the hearts of those he wished to change. Instead, he used non-violence, which highlighted the violence used against his people. He awakened the outrage of the powerful. In such ways are changes begun. King stated in his "Letter from a Birmingham Jail" that nonviolence was the only answer to hate and that instead of seeking victory and humiliation over our enemies we should instead seek friendship.

As American Christians, though, we don't want to talk about giving up power, about divesting ourselves of privilege. We think we have a better way called leadership. Leadership is a visionary who gets other people to follow and accomplish his or her vision. It's highly Individualistic. The church at this moment in history talks a lot about leadership and about building leaders. In one recent week, I received twenty-two invitations to attend conferences.

Seventeen of those were leadership conferences: how to become a better leader, how to get a board of leaders, how to train leaders, how to develop leaders. But out of the twenty-two invitations I received, not one was on how to become a servant. You can learn how to become a "servant-leader," but that's significantly different from becoming a servant.

For all the issues found in our nation, Jesus Christ calls us to the center. That's the answer, that's where we find resolution to these battles between powerful and powerless, conservative and liberal, Individualistic and Enmeshed.

If wholeness is found in the center, in giving up the self, how does that look for each of the issues we've discussed? Most of the country is closer to the center than to the extremes. But the fact is, most of the country has checked out, in all these fights. They're tired of being pulled to the extremes. It's the people in the center, though, that can pull us to the center. Once you check out, all you're left with is the fight. So how do we bring the people back? How do we make it worthwhile for people to come back?

The gospel is the answer. We haven't been taken out of the world. And yet, for many people that's what we've done on all these issues. We've lost influence and so we've opted out of the fight. The gospel, though, is about influence and bringing about change.

## The Loss of Influence

With the kind of breakdown the church has had into the same Individualistic/Enmeshed extremes that have plagued the rest of our society, how will the church handle the issues facing it? A good example is with the question of homosexual marriages. How should the church handle it at a place of wholeness rather than extremes?

When we come to the center, when we give up power, we find ourselves at the foot of the cross. We need, therefore, to look at the issues from that perspective. Life at the foot of the cross looks entirely different. I believe that it would encompass the message of Micah 6:8: "What does the Lord require of you? To act justly and to love mercy and to walk humbly with your God."

While I don't have room here to go into the depths of this theological gem, I want to touch on the issue of justice. We may talk in the church about loving mercy – and that's questionable when the issue is homosexuality – and we try to be humble before God, but we don't do much justice in the church. At Iliff School of Theology at a recent Hispanic conference, which embraced a multiplicity of mainline and evangelical denominations, I had the privilege of summarizing the events of the day. We talked about Individualism and Community, and whether we could have true community when we're living the American Dream. I brought up the question that I brought up earlier in this book: is gay marriage destroying the family or is the American Dream destroying the family? Eventually, a Pentecostal gentleman got up and said, "Brother Perea, I appreciate your thinking. It's radical thinking, and it's thinking we need to be doing, but I have to bring you back to the essence of the Bible, and the Bible says that homosexuality is wrong. It's an abomination and we need to clearly say that and not water it down."

Let me make my position clear. I'm not suggesting that we water down sin. There's been enough of that going on in our country. What I am suggesting is that we put the fact that there are kids in this country going to bed hungry tonight on the same level, even par, with the fact that there are gays committing sodomy tonight. When the church addresses those two with that kind of voice about sin, then I think we have something to say about this issue. But until we do that, I don't think we have anything to say.

We have become reactionaries and speak only to hot-button issues. I asked the gentleman, "Have you preached against homosexuality or done a series on it?" He said yes. I said, "Have you ever done a series on hunger in America?" He said no. In other words, we're willing to discuss the sin of homosexuality, but we won't discuss the sin of ignoring poverty in the midst of our McDonald's obsessed obesity. As long as you're willing to do one but not the other, you're missing the boat.

We can't pick and choose which sins to address. We have lost relevance, lost our influence, by picking issues instead of addressing sin. We cannot demand that people listen to us if we're not willing to address all sin equally. There are many more heterosexual people involved in sex outside of marriage than homosexual, and how are we going to deal with that? Wholeness is found at the foot of the cross, and at the foot of the cross there is no room for picking and choosing.

## An Example of Wholeness

In order to come to wholeness, each side must give up power. An example of this can be found in education. It's going to take Outcome Based Education along with Back to Basics to reach wholeness in education. Learning styles are different and we need to teach both. It's not either/or. We need to speak to the heart and the head, facts and feelings. Both. Each side needs to come to an understanding, to be cognizant of the other side. There must be a way to find a middle ground between public and private schools and the issue of vouchers.

"Good Schools Pennsylvania" has a mission geared toward promoting public schools. It notes that even with private education and vouchers, fully 80 percent of students will still receive a public education. Part of their mission to improve public schools is to have higher expectations, smaller class sizes, accountability, and extra help available in the form of tutoring, summer classes, etc. Through these efforts, federal money will be distributed more equitably among the school districts. They realize, though, that they can't do it alone. And certain churches in Pennsylvania are realizing the same thing. Bishop Roy Almquist with the Southeastern PA Synod Evangelical Lutheran church in America partners with Good Schools Pennsylvania. He notes on their website:

> One of our desires is to activate the people of faith within the Commonwealth of Pennsylvania to see the issue of the education of our children as truly a spiritual issue, as a justice issue, as an issue that should involve all decent people of faith. We only get one shot at our children. We can't go back and do it over. This is the moment. This is the time. The challenge of preparing our children for a technologically advancing society is a critical one. And we need to do it now.[2]

Paul Vallas, the former Chicago schools superintendent, found the same thing.

> From combating delinquency to boosting academic achievement, [Vallas] is proving that the best way to reform public education is to replicate the successes of religious schools. . . . Vallas' three-year campaign to involve churches and synagogues in the lives

of schoolchildren has recruited about 300 congregations. They provide tutors, after-school programs, safe havens and even classroom space in their churches to relieve overcrowding. Despite the naysaying of church-state lawyers, the number of public educators who view religious communities as essential to rescuing failing schools is growing.[3]

Another excellent example of a move toward wholeness, this time in the political realm, happened earlier in 2003. Alabama governor Bob Riley, a Republican with an amazing track record of opposing liberal legislation, tried pushing a tax reform plan through the Alabama Legislature that would shift the state's tax burden off the poor and onto wealthy individuals and corporations. His reason, he said, was Christian theology. "I've spent a lot of time studying the New Testament, and it has three philosophies: love God, love each other, and take care of the least among you. I don't think anyone can justify putting an income tax on someone who makes $4,600 a year."[4]

Unfortunately, the voters did not ratify the plan. However, Riley made his point. As pointed out by The New York Times, "Alabama's tax-reform crusade is posing a pointed question to the Christian Coalition, Focus on the Family and other groups that seek to import Christian values into national policy: If Jesus were active in politics today, wouldn't he be lobbying for the poor?"[5]

When a Republican goes against the Individualistic dream, putting aside his party's idea of power, in order to help the powerless, that's a tremendous move toward wholeness.

# Conclusion: Wake Up!

Throughout the course of these reflections about the "New America," I have shown how the reluctance of people on the Individualistic extreme and people on the Enmeshed extreme to work together has greatly intensified our nation's ills. I have also spoken of how the church, sadly, has fallen prey to this same division. Yet I remain hopeful that the church will learn to be of like mind with Christ and come to care more deeply about spreading the gospel than preserving itself. I will present my ideas about how the church can be restored to its true mission in another book.

We're going to have to deal with the issues rather than the ideologies. We're going to have to realize that it takes both sides to come to the center. Left vs right, conservative vs liberal, capitalist vs communalist, outcome based vs back to basics, Individualistic vs Enmeshed.

Most people are more centrist in their views. The problem is that they've gotten so tired of the fight, so tired of the pull from the extremes, that they've opted out. The more the extremes pull, the more apathetic people become.

If it is only the people at the center who can bring balance, if it is only the people at the center who can pull the extremes together, then we the people need to throw off our apathy and become involved. What we need to do is to wake up.

## Notes

[1] Manuel Ortiz, "Seeking the Kingdom in Our Cities," *The Banner,* Feb. 28, 2000, 28.

[2] http://www.goodschoolspa.org/faith/

[3] Joe Loconte, "Let's make religion public schools' ally," *USA Today*, Nov. 11, 1999.

[4] Adam Cohen, "What Would Jesus Do? Sock It to Alabama's Corporate Landowners," *New York Times*, June 10, 2003.

[5] Ibid.